Keepin' It Real

Integrating new literacies with effective classroom practice

Lisa Donohue

Foreword: David Booth

Pembroke Publishers Limited

To the special people in my life, who have given me my roots,
and given me my wings.

© **2010 Pembroke Publishers**
538 Hood Road
Markham, Ontario, Canada L3R 3K9
www.pembrokepublishers.com

Distributed in the U.S. by Stenhouse Publishers
480 Congress Street
Portland, ME 04101
www.stenhouse.com

All rights reserved.
No part of this publication may be reproduced in any form or by any means electronic
or mechanical, including photocopy, scanning, recording, or any information, stor-
age or retrieval system, without permission in writing from the publisher. Pages of this
publication designated as reproducible with the following icon ✍ may be reproduced
under licence from Access Copyright.

Every effort has been made to contact copyright holders for permission to reproduce
borrowed material. The publishers apologize for any such omissions and will be pleased
to rectify them in subsequent reprints of the book.

We acknowledge the financial support of the Government of Canada through the Book
Publishing Industry Development Program (BPIDP) for our publishing activities.

We acknowledge the assistance of the Government of Ontario through the Ontario
Media Development Corporation's Ontario Book Initiative.

Library and Archives Canada Cataloguing in Publication

Donohue, Lisa
    Keepin' it real : integrating new literacies with effective classroom
practice / Lisa Donohue.

Includes index.
ISBN 978-1-55138-260-9

    1. Language arts (Elementary). 2. English language—Study and
teaching (Elementary). 3. Media literacy. 4. Digital media. 5. Social
media. 6. Critical thinking—Study and teaching (Elementary).
I. Title. II. Title: Keeping it real.

LB1576.7.D75 2010   372.6'044   C2010-903835-5

Editor: Kat Mototsune
Cover Design: John Zehethofer
Typesetting: Jay Tee Graphics Ltd.

Printed and bound in Canada
9 8 7 6 5 4 3 2 1

FSC
Mixed Sources
Product group from well-managed
forests and other controlled sources
Cert no. SW-COC-002358
www.fsc.org
© 1996 Forest Stewardship Council

Contents

Foreword

Over the past few years, I have become a colleague and friend of Lisa Donohue, and I have had the good fortune to see a true professional educator at work. Lisa is an astute teacher/researcher, observing her students with a keen eye, searching for best practices that will support their development, reading every applicable book and journal article to deepen her knowledge base, and then demonstrating and articulating her strategies by writing practical, theoretically sound books for teachers. We have worked together on several teacher conferences and, each time I have listened to her presentations, she has moved forward in her own thinking—beginning with reading instruction, then writing support, and now literacy and technology. When I read her professional books, what impresses me most is the clarity of thought she brings to each of these complex instructional areas. I marvel at the concise ways in which she turns theory into practice, how she embeds what contemporary research offers us into manageable units of information that teachers can incorporate into their classrooms tomorrow.

In her latest book, *Keepin' It Real*, Lisa takes on the world of technology and its relationship to literacy, both inside and outside school. This field of research has been a particular interest of mine for the last ten years, and she has not only investigated the connections we, as teachers, are making to its role in supporting reading and writing development, she has also organized those aspects in useful and pertinent categories, and then added classroom experiences and events that encourage and enable teachers to implement a variety of forms and formats into their daily programs. The section on Putting It All Together offers every teacher a way to enter this new world of literacy, depending on the school's resources and potential for integrating digital literacies into classroom practice.

Lisa Donohue writes alongside teachers, inviting them to join the global classroom, offering them ways in, free of admonition and guilt. She knows how to support each of us in our own inquiries, shining light on what may seem to be complicated new educational processes, so that we can extend our own capacities as educators, and help our children prepare for a world of literacy that changes almost daily, as strong interpreters and constructors of a variety of text forms on page and on screen. Her book will be a welcome addition and support to my own work on digital literacies, and I shall share it with everyone I meet.

David Booth
Chair of The Centre for Literacy
The Schulich School of Education, Nipissing University

Introduction

Reflection is an amazing thing: We can truly understand the direction we need to go in only by looking at the direction from which we have come. This is not a new concept. In fact, Christopher Columbus navigated the Atlantic by a process called *dead reckoning*. Using the stars and early navigational tools, he used his knowledge of where he had been, combined with the direction and distance he had traveled, to determine where he was, and indeed where he was to go. Although his destination was unknown, and technically he didn't end up at the destination he'd initially planned, he had a good idea of the direction he needed to go to get closer to his goal. Teaching is a reflective process. We are facing the future every day and, like Christopher Columbus sailing across the Atlantic, we may know where we've come from, but we certainly don't know our final destination or what the future will hold. As educators, we gain a glimpse of the future as we prepare our students to enter it. Our youngsters are the ones who will define the worlds to come, and our role is to equip them as well as possible for the unknown future.

As I continue to reflect on my teaching, I'm constantly asking myself to justify my practice. Why do I do the things I do? What is the intention behind the tasks I ask my students to complete? Am I ensuring that they are participating in authentic learning situations? How can I maximize their engagement, their risk-taking, their motivation? How can I develop students who are self-directed, goal-setting, autonomous learners who will face the future head-on? Who will question, criticize, analyze, and evaluate the world in which they live?

The world is changing so rapidly, so too must my teaching practice. Would you be comfortable being treated by a doctor who refused to heed technological advances in his field? The field of medicine, like the world of literacy, is one that is making dramatic advances on a daily basis. It is the way we bring these new innovations to life in our classrooms that will enhance the learning of our students. The children of this generation live in a digital world, embracing everything digital. The way they interact with their digital world determines new forms of literacy. The world is filled with "new literacies." What does that mean for the "old literacies"? Do we disregard everything old and replace it with the new? But how is it possible for the new literacies to exist in a world without the old? How can we separate the old from the new? The "old" literacies—reading, writing, speaking, listening—are inextricably woven into the "new" literacies—digital literacy, social literacy, media literacy, critical literacy.

It is impossible to understand and interact using new forms of literacy unless we are proficient in the foundations of communication. In order to proficiently use technological advances, one must be skilled at reading and writing. In order to utilize social networking tools, one must understand the basics of communication—speaking and listening. The world may be changing, the tools we use to interact with it evolving, but the basic skills we need to actively engage in it remain constant.

The relationship between the new literacies and the old is one of mutual benefit. Students need to have strong reading and writing skills in order to develop these other literacies. The foundations of literacy are not changing. In fact, more than ever, it is important that students can read, understand, and evaluate the information they read. It is equally important that students develop strong writing skills so they will be able to actively engage with others through the written word. Students need to listen to others, articulate their own thoughts, and understand the different ways in which we communicate with each other. The new literacies are completely grounded in the foundations of reading, writing, listening, and speaking.

As educators, we are preparing our students for the future. We are equipping them with skills that will be essential as they graduate and enter the workforce. However, these skills are evolving. No longer will it be sufficient for students to read and write, but they will need to read, write, analyze, create, discover, learn and relearn on a daily basis. They will need to examine the world in which they live, connect with others, and apply knowledge in new and innovative ways. According to Daniel Pink (2005),

> The last few decades have belonged to a certain kind of person with a certain kind of mind—computer programmers who could crank code, lawyers who could craft contracts, MBAs who could crunch numbers. But the keys to the kingdom are changing hands. The future belongs to a very different kind of person with a very different kind of mind—creators and empathizers, pattern recognizers, and meaning makers. These people—artists, inventors, designers, storytellers, caregivers, consolers, big picture thinkers—will now reap society's richest rewards and share its greatest joys.

As the world evolves, we must prepare our students to embrace these new changes. We need to teach them to be flexible, adaptable adults. They need to think critically, analyze deeply, and create effectively.

This book is intended to help educators navigate through the new literacies and find meaningful connections through all learning experiences. As 21st-century learners, our students no longer see learning as separate subject areas, but rather perceive it as a web of interconnected ideas and concepts. The new literacies are not separate from all other forms of learning, but instead are new approaches for interacting with the subject matter. Students cannot be digitally literate in isolation, but need to be digitally literate about the things they are learning. Similarly, they cannot be media literate, critically literate, or socially literate without having meaningful material with which to interact. Using the new literacies, students are able to gain a deeper understanding of information, can critically analyze the things they encounter, and are aptly equipped to respond in unique and creative ways.

Throughout this book, you will meet dynamic educators who are embracing the new literacies to the fullest. In the Evolution in Action boxes and through real quotes from students, you will see how 21st-century students are thriving through the integration of digital tools in their daily learning. Keep It Real activities show in a classroom setting the importance of using technology as a tool, rather than a subject. As a catalyst for thought, Digital Task Cards clearly illustrate the ways in which teachers can bring digital tools into their curriculum.

These cards connect directly to subject matter learned in reading, writing, math, science, and social studies.

As educators, we are all tasked with finding innovative ways to deliver our curriculum in a way that will engage, challenge, and motivate all learners. The new literacies allow us to use a broader range of tools, strategies, and approaches that will broaden students understanding, deepen their thinking, and expand their application of the material they learn.

CHAPTER ONE

Literacies Old and New

"If we teach today as we did yesterday, we rob our children of tomorrow."
—John Dewey

Starting with What We Know

Literacy, by definition, is the ability to read, write, and communicate effectively with others. Any form of literacy assumes some level of proficiency in reading, writing, listening, and speaking. These literacies must be considered foundational for all subsequent literacies. In order to interact with others through a wide range of communication tools, we first must be able to read, write, listen, and speak. Without a solid foundation in these core literacies, one would meet with little success in newer literacies, whatever they might be.

Effective readers need to be able to read a variety of text forms for a variety of purposes. They select texts and locate information. Proficient readers use a wide range of strategies to decode and comprehend text. They read fiction and nonfiction, and are intuitively knowledgeable about which is which. Readers engage with texts, they question the things they read, they make inferences and draw conclusions. They visualize images in their minds using all of their senses. An effective reader knows what's important and what's not. They're able to make predictions and think critically about the things they are reading. Readers are also aware of the different forms texts can take. They recognize instantly the different features of a poem or a letter, they read a newspaper differently from the way they read a recipe, and they automatically switch their minds from understanding the imaginary world of fiction to the reality of nonfiction.

Effective writers are able to write for a variety of purposes and for a variety of audiences. They recognize which text form is suitable for a given purpose. Proficient writers are able to capture their ideas in a way that they can be shared with others. They have an understanding of audience and write differently depending on who will be reading their work. As writers, they consider things like the form of writing, the content of the piece, the audience who will read it. They think about things like conventions, voice, and word choice. Writers may choose to write a list of items, compose a letter to a friend, and respond to an e-mail, all within a short period of time. They don't stop to think about the form the communication will take; they automatically know how to best capture their ideas and share them with others.

Listening and speaking are skills that are essential for communicating effectively with others. Students learn to listen and consider the ideas of others, and share their own thinking in articulate ways. They learn to analyze and question the words of others. They learn to read nonverbal cues like facial expressions, tone of voice, and body language. Likewise, they learn how to effectively use these cues to express their own thoughts. Students learn to negotiate and take turns, they learn work cooperatively with others, and they learn to engage in conversations with their peers.

Evolution in Action

My good friend Arthur Birenbaum told me that teaching is the only profession where we have the same responsibilities on our first day as on our last. It's the way in which we carry out these responsibilities that define our career. If we're doing the same thing we did 20 years ago, then we have failed not only ourselves, but our students too. Teaching is evolution in action. We are constantly redefining the ways in which we do our jobs. We are reflecting on our practice and evaluating our effectiveness. It is this constant reflection that causes us to change, grow, and evolve.

Our students are living in a fast-paced world of electronics and technological devices. They are processing more information at a faster rate than imaginable. As teachers we need to adapt to the changing world in which we all live. It is not enough to teach our students to read, write, listen, and speak. They need to know how to read and write for authentic purposes. We need to teach them how to become digitally literate, socially literate, media literate, and critically literate. They need to connect with the world and question the information they encounter; they need to analyze, evaluate, and think for themselves. They need to interact with others in real, authentic, engaging ways.

How do we interact with the world? Although the form of communication is evolving, we depend heavily on our existing literacies to interpret and share information. We need to be able to read a variety of text forms and communicate using writing. We need to listen to others and to speak, clearly articulating our thoughts. The old literacies are foundational for success with the new, and the new literacies (when used effectively) serve to strengthen and support students' reading, writing, listening, and speaking.

Digital literacy is the ability to use, locate, understand, evaluate, and organize information using digital tools. It enables users to connect to the world, communicate with others, collaborate with others, and create using a variety of media forms. It allows students to consolidate their learning and encourages them to critically analyze the information they encounter. Students who are digitally literate use technology as a tool to support their learning. They are engaged in authentic experiences that extend beyond their classrooms.

Media literacy is the ability to analyze, evaluate, and interpret messages that are conveyed through different forms of communications. Literacy in this area promotes the critical analysis of messages. Students ask questions like these: Who created the message? For whom was the message intended? In what way is the message biased? Whose voice is being heard? Whose voice is being silenced? What strategies are being used to engage an audience? Media literacy encourages students to consider messages from different perspectives, to think critically about the content, form, and meaning. When students are literate in this area, they are able to understand, evaluate, and create a wide range of media messages.

Social literacy is the ability to connect and communicate with those around you. Students who are socially literate are able to adapt their behavior to suit

The new literacies:
- digital literacy
- media literacy
- social literacy
- critical literacy

a range of situations. They recognize the subtleties of body language, tone of voice, facial expressions, and gestures. Students can use their understanding of social literacy to interact with others in positive ways. This is not a new concept. Social skills, etiquette, and manners have been valued and taught for many years. However, as social communications move into the digital realm, these skills are becoming more relevant as an aspect of literacy. Establishing norms for responsible citizenship, effective communication, and respectful interactions is an important consideration when students are working collaboratively. Most recently, these aspects of social skills are fitting under the umbrella of literacy. If the definition of literacy is to be able to read, write, and communicate effectively with others, then, in order to do so, we must use social literacy as a way of mediating these interactions. Students need to select their words carefully, think of the ways their message will be interpreted, and make important decisions about appropriate ways to respond when they may be in a difficult situation. Students who are socially literate are able to make responsible decisions when interacting with others, both face-to-face and online.

Critical literacy is the ability to analyze written information to evaluate the underlying messages. Readers who are critically literate are not only able to read and make sense of written text, but they are also able to engage in a discussion with others about its meaning. They are able to state their opinion and use information from a text to support their thinking. Critically literate individuals reflect on the information they encounter and consider the impact it has on their own lives. They question what they read and evaluate the accuracy. They consider the source of the information and the way it connects to their prior knowledge, opinions, and perceptions. Critical literacy is not a new concept. For many years we have been encouraging young readers to think, evaluate, and analyze the texts they read. However, critical literacy is becoming more of a focus for youngsters as we expand the parameters of the texts they encounter. Critical literacy is not a new literacy, solely arising out of the use of technology; however, the use of technology has increased the importance of teaching students to become critically literate.

Immediate Feedback = Immediate Change

There are few tools that bring about an immediate change in student behavior. However, when I introduced one of my students to a new digital recording tool, within minutes I saw instant results. This youngster had great difficulty articulating his words when he spoke, especially when he read. He would slur all of the words together, making it extremely difficult to monitor his reading. He also found it difficult to speak with varying volumes and intonation. One day, we made a huge breakthrough. Using a digital voice recorder, we recorded his reading. He read one sentence at a time, playing it back and listening to his own words. He was surprised by the fact that he, too, was unable to understand what he was saying. Together we recorded his reading sentence by sentence, listening to each phase individually and rerecording if it was unclear. Once he had recorded a few sentences, we listened to them together—to discover that he was, this time, reading with deliberate breaks between words. The digital recording tool represented his speech in a visual way, and he discovered that he could actually see the breaks between his words. Within minutes, he was speaking more articulately and clearly, and he had even started introducing inflection into his reading. Later, when we gathered his peers together and replayed the digital recording, he was thrilled, for the first time in his life, to "read" a story to the class.

How then do the new literacies affect these foundational ones? Students who experience more authentic opportunities for sharing and applying their learning are more engaged. Digital tools allow for the extension of these foundational literacies. For example, writers could use a wiki to collaborate when writing a newspaper (see Digital Task Card: Class Newspaper on page 30), readers could use a blog as a forum for responding to their books (see Digital Task Card: Online Reading Response Journal on page 34), and students can use a chatroom as a way of having a conversation about the information they are learning (see Digital Task Card: Book Talk on page 16).

See Digital Task Card: Book Talk on page 16.

Keep It Real

A group of Grade 3 students used a chatroom to post book recommendations for each other. They shared information about the books they were reading or had recently completed. They were careful to include enough information to "hook" a potential reader, while not giving too much away. The chat format helped them keep their ideas short and succinct. Often students had read the same books, and the conversation continued on a deeper level. They shared their predictions, their connections, and their inferences. The chatroom was the perfect forum for their conversations.

When students have a broader audience for their writing, they write more. They recognize that their writing has direct impact on others. The quality of what they write matters, because they know it will influence the response they get. As students engage more with others through digital tools, they will encounter additional written forms. Through the exposure to a wider array of text forms, students will become more versatile writers. They will begin to determine the form that will best convey their message and explore new and innovative ways of expressing their ideas.

Through new literacies, students are constantly being challenged to stretch their reading abilities. They encounter different text forms, media presentations, and social communications. Students need to read, understand, and analyze a vast array of information. Text forms are changing and evolving, but the skills we use to interact with them remain the same. It is ever more important that we teach students to think while they read and not only decode the words on the page.

Finally, listening and speaking are the foundational skills for every social interaction. Students need to communicate effectively with others using the norms of social interactions. They need to use appropriate voice (when speaking or writing) and attend to the ideas of others. Digital tools allow students to connect and communicate with others well beyond their classrooms. They are able to listen, speak, and collaborate, regardless of physical boundaries.

In summary, reading, writing, listening, and speaking are foundational for the development of the newer literacies, and the new literacies, when used effectively, serve to strengthen, support, and bring purpose to reading, writing, and communicating.

Evolution in Action

A leader in 21st-century education, Royan Lee feels that, in order to equip our students for success in the future, they need to effectively read, write, and communicate in the digital world.

© 2010 Royan Lee and Bitstrips.

Tech Tool: Chatroom
What is a chatroom?
A chatroom is an online space where users can have a conversation.

Digital Task Card: Book Talk

Use a chatroom to have conversations about the books you are reading. You might choose to share books that you think other people in the chatroom may enjoy, and you might be interested to hear book recommendations from others.

When you're sharing information about the book you are reading, think about how you can make the book sound appealing to others without giving too much away.

You can start by asking questions: "Does anyone like books with lots of adventure?" or "Has anyone read a really funny book lately?"

You need to know the title of the book and the author in order to recommend it to others. You might choose to share a very brief summary of the plot—but not too much. Remember it is a chat, not a speech. You need to keep your ideas short and succinct.

Ask lots of questions of the other members in the chatroom—you might discover new books that you can't wait to read.

Pembroke Publishers. © 2010 *Keepin' It Real* by Lisa Donohue. ISBN 978-1-55138-260-9

CHAPTER TWO

Digital Literacy

"Go out on a limb. That's where the fruit is."
—Jimmy Carter

Get Plugged In

See www.commoncraft.com/show for ideas on introducing complex subjects to your students.

Digital literacy is possibly one of the scariest topics for many teachers. Imagine teaching a subject in which the students know more than the teacher—that's the world of digital literacy. Once we accept this simple truth, we are more able to approach our role with different purpose. Marc Prensky (2001) refers to the children of this generation as "digital natives"—they have spent their entire lives surrounded by digital tools—and those of us who have watched technology evolve around us are "digital immigrants." The children of this generation are "wired" differently. They approach the technological world with a confidence and fluency that many adults struggle with. Children are fearless when it comes to trying new tools. The truth is, there are few classrooms where the teacher knows more about the digital tools than the students. How then, can we "teach" them anything? What is the point of introducing digital literacies into the classroom, if the students are already the experts? Students may be innately comfortable with the use of the technology, but they need guidance in using it to strengthen their understanding of the world. Students often lack the critical reasoning skills to evaluate various digital information.

In no way do I claim to be a digital expert. In fact, there are so many different applications and tools I'm unfamiliar with that it's frightening to think of weighing the known against the unknown. But that's the digital world. We are constantly asking our students to take risks as learners. Leaping into the world of digital literacy means that we, as teachers, may need to take more risks. It's never easy to try something new, especially when we have an audience of youngsters who are obviously more comfortable with the tools than we are, and who are eager to give advice, too often in a loud, embarrassing manner.

So why take the risk? Why introduce students to a wide range of digital tools? Why should we subject ourselves to the possibility of the public humiliation of having our students correct us in front of the class? The students are more than willing to help us navigate this world. If we approach digital literacy with the understanding that our students are the natives and we are the immigrants, we can all learn together. When introducing students to any new digital tool, I make the point of telling them that this is what I know about the tool, and of asking them that when they've learned more, to please share it with me.

Digital literacy allows students to apply their reading, writing, speaking, and listening skills in authentic learning situations. It encourages them to move beyond the classroom and into the world. Through digital tools, students are able to connect, communicate, create, collaborate, consolidate, and critically analyze. They become more globally aware, more proactive, and more engaged.

Connect

Digital tools allow students to connect with the world without leaving their classroom. They can go on virtual field trips; they can examine images from the other side of the world. They can read, listen, watch, and experience things well beyond the boundaries of any classroom environment. Students can research events in real time; they can experience history as it happens. They no longer need to be passive observers of the world around them. They are able to connect to the world, communicate with others, and add their voices to issues as they happen. Through digital tools, students are able to participate in world events and affect others with their actions.

Imagine being able to bring your students to the water's edge after a catastrophic oil spill, sharing images of the wildlife, the coastline, and the massive attempts to minimize the damage. What if you could take your students to the middle of the Pacific Ocean and see first-hand the vast collection of garbage and debris that is collecting in the Pacific Gyre? Imagine visiting an earthquake-ravaged city, looking into the faces of the innocent victims, hearing their voices, coming together as a global community. Students can travel to unimaginable places at the click of a button. Children are more than ever able to "think globally and act locally."

After the catastrophic disaster of the 2009 earthquake in Haiti that destroyed the capital city Port au Prince, many teachers were able to share the magnitude of this disaster with their students. Haiti did not need to seem like such a distant place, a small remote country on the island of Hispaniola. Although it might be hundreds of miles away, Haiti was easily connected with these classrooms through the Internet. As students read about the earthquake, they started to ask questions about the science behind earthquakes, the geography of the tectonic plates. They wondered about the Richter scale. Although they did not speak the same language, the students were able to hear the stories of the victims. Students could access immediate answers to their questions—moving from thinking about the wide-scale disaster to the immediate action that needed to be taken. The more time the students spent reading about the disaster, the more their questions moved from scientific and geographical ones to questions about action. They started to wonder what they could do. Because these students were connected to the world, they saw the rescue efforts in action. They saw things like mobile tent hospitals and wondered how much they cost. Students saw simple water purifiers and questioned their availability to the survivors. Although they were a world away, the students knew exactly how they could participate immediately in the relief efforts. They were connected. They experienced world events in real time and were active in bringing about relief. Children who are connected through digital tools see themselves as having immediate impact on the world. The feeling of helplessness that could come out of the vastness of the situation was greatly reduced. Within hours of the devastating earthquake, students in many schools initiated fundraising efforts. They were well-equipped with knowledge. They knew who they needed to help, how they could help, and exactly what it would cost.

"The Internet connects our classroom to the entire world. We're able to know what's happening in the real-world while we're in school."
—Phillip (Grade 6)

Communicate

Can you imagine living in a world without the telephone? Wouldn't you feel isolated and cut off from the rest of the world? We need to know that we have the ability to communicate with others, not only those in the same room as us, but also those well beyond the walls. Why do we need to communicate with others? Is it to gather information? Share information? Collaborate? The simple answer: yes.

Students share this need to communicate with others. They communicate with their families, their peers, and their friends. They speak, they listen, they negotiate. When students use tools like wikis, blogs, and chatrooms, they are able to communicate with others. They can have their voices heard and can listen to the voices of others. The digital world is the great equalizer—everyone's voice is valued. Even students who often find it difficult to express their views rise to the challenge of the digital world. Often children find confidence in the keys of a computer, finding the words to express their thoughts. They can question others, provide an opinion, or give feedback to another learner.

Communication is a skill that takes into account the context of a situation and the content of the dialogue. We recognize that we recount the details of a significant event in our lives differently when communicating for different audiences. We change the way in which we choose to express ourselves depending on the medium through which we are communicating. Students need to develop a familiarity with the different norms affiliated with various forms of communication. Students can use blogs to express their opinions of various subjects, wikis to collaborate and share their ideas with others, and chats to engage in a conversation with their peers. Communication is an essential skill, and the media through which we communicate are evolving on a seemingly daily basis. Students need to understand the wide array of communication tools, forms, and applications that are available to them.

During high school and university, I remember sitting in large auditoriums or gymnasiums to write final exams. The instructions were clear. There was to be no talking during the test. Students caught cheating would immediately have their tests removed from them, and they would receive an automatic zero. I remember writing frantically, as the sound of the instructor's heavy shoes paced up and down the long aisles of students. Too often, students attempted to communicate with each other in hushed whispers or by passing tiny notes one to another.

Now, communication during a test situation is faster, clearer, and much simpler. In a few seconds, students can send text messages from one cell phone to another, receiving an instant reply. Cheating? Yes. But how do we stop it? If we are constantly re-evaluating and rethinking our teaching practice for ways to align our classroom with real life, we need to examine this form of testing. I challenge you to think back through your life. When—other than at school—have you had to sit in a room, in complete isolation, and recall everything you know about a certain subject? We want students to know where to find the information and what to do with it once they access it. What we need to be assessing in our students is not the recall of the information, but the application of it. Consider this mindshift: from knowing the information, to knowing *what to do with* the information. Our kids live in the information age. Information is cheap—knowledge is power. This is a fundamental change in our approach to assessing student learning.

www.twitter.com

Evolution in Action

A teacher who is leading the way with this new way of thinking is Royan Lee. Royan teaches a Grade 6 class, and not only encourages his students to communicate during a test, but also shows them how. Royan uses a process called *backchanneling*. Backchanneling is a way for students to engage in a conversation about their learning while they are learning. Royan uses Twitter to allow students to chat during instructional time, even during tests. Facing head-on the reality that students live in a communication age, he has fully embraced their communication skills. Royan has taught students how to question his instructions, respond to the inquiries of others, provide feedback to their peers, and support each other's learning. Instead of forbidding students to communicate, he has enriched their learning by providing them an appropriate forum in which to communicate, taught them how to use this communication effectively, and set very clear expectations about what communications are appropriate.

Instead of thinking that some children are going to "cheat," why not use the opportunity as an acceptable medium for learning? In this way, the teacher is able to monitor the communications that are taking place in a forum that is acceptable and accountable. If we provide students with the venue for these communications, if we legitimize them, all of a sudden communicating is no longer a "bad" thing. The teacher would have access to students' conversations and be able to assess not only the content of the test, but also the content of students' communication with each other. These communications would give as much, if not more, insight into the students' learning. Imagine a class where students are allowed and encouraged to communicate with each other about their learning! What if, instead of resisting students' need to communicate, we embraced it, we fostered it, we supported it, and we used it for their benefit?

Create

Creativity is directly linked to inspiration, and inspiration is directly linked to engagement. When students are engaged in a task, they are more motivated and creative. Students who are using digital tools to create new and innovative ways of sharing their learning will take greater risks and demonstrate more perseverance than their peers. Engaging learners with digital tools helps them create and synthesize the information they are learning about. Students are able to find inspiration through the integration of creative approaches.

See Digital Task Card: Book Soundtrack on page 28.

Evolution in Action

Peter Jenkins is one of the most creative, innovative teachers I have ever met. He is constantly looking for authentic ways in which to engage students and promote integration of literacy, technology, and the arts. In his Grade 7 class, his students were reading a modernized and simplified version of the play *Romeo and Juliet*. These students approached the text in a unique way and began finding creative ways of expressing their understanding. They analyzed the mood of the various scenes and the pace of the action. The students were tasked with the challenge of creating the soundtrack for the story: *Imagine being the director of the onstage production. What would the music sound like? What mood would the various scenes convey?* Using a simple digital mixing software application, these students made the play come alive through music. Peter continued this integration of arts and literacy by having the students design the CD case. Each student wrote a brief explanation about how the music they had created related to the scene from the play, and outlined the events taking place during their piece. Wouldn't this have made the play come alive in the classroom?! These students were so engaged, they volunteered to work through recess, during lunch, and after school, dedicating much of their free time to this creative task

By creating unique learning opportunities, you not only make learning exciting and engaging, but you also allow students to experiment with new forms of expression. They can take risks like never before because, with this type of learning, there is no wrong answer.

Collaborate

Evolution in Action

Jonathan Lewis is a dynamic and innovative teacher. His students collaborate both within his class and with students in other classes. In once such instance, he partnered with fellow teacher Ming Huang in a neighboring school. The students in the two classes had been learning about persuasive techniques through listening, speaking, and writing. Jonathan and Ming created a number of possible debate topics and students selected the one that most appealed to them. Rather than pitting one school against the other in the debate, these teachers chose to foster collaboration. Students in Jonathan's class partnered with students in Ming's class to research information, share ideas. and formulate their arguments. They communicated through chats and wikis, working collaboratively to compile their work. This activity culminated in an online debate, with students connected through a video streaming link. While one member of a team voiced an argument, their partners were able to provide the debater with information through backchanneling. This was online collaboration to the max! This massive collaborative effort taught students the importance of sharing their ideas in clear and concise ways. They found ways of researching together, validating each other's thinking, and supporting the learning of their peers.

Using digital tools, students are able to collaborate with each other in new and innovative ways. In a digital-rich learning environment, students are able to connect with others, sharing their work in many different ways. Imagine if students could work collaboratively between schools—even if the schools were in different cities, or different countries. What if these students were able to work together in real time, contributing ideas to a shared piece of work?

Collaborative learning transcends the boundaries of the classroom. Students can collaborate with anyone, anywhere, anytime. Imagine the possibilities!

Consolidate

On a daily basis, we work with students to develop their reading, writing, and thinking skills. We introduce them to different forms of writing and a broad range of genres of texts. But students are often limited by the parameters we set around their assignments. We choose the theme, we set expectations, we set limits. Learning is most powerful when students are able to use their knowledge in unique and innovative ways. Students who are able to apply their learning and transfer it to new situations are synthesizing all of the skills they are developing in the classroom. We need to constantly look for opportunities for our students to consolidate their learning. They need a way of putting it all together.

Our goal as educators is for our students to begin to apply their learning to a wide range of situations. We hope that the skills they develop in the classroom will be transferred to real life. Imagine discovering that your students were so engaged in literacy that they had formed their own secret society of writers. Imagine that these students had independently identified their own strengths and took on personalized roles that best suited their skills. What if they took the initiative to create a virtual world where fictional characters lived? A world where they wrote, shared, supported, and nurtured each other's literacy skills?

Evolution in Action

Teacher Farhana Panju has always been a forward-thinker when it comes to digital literacy; however, she was taken aback when one of her students invited her to visit his website. He had started a blog page where a fictional character came to life. As Farhana perused the site, she discovered that more than half of her students were active users of the blog. One student had created a theme song and another had assumed the role of the designer—together the students were collaborating to create something amazing. Her students had consolidated their learning and created numerous episodes of exciting adventures. Students provided feedback to each other; they wrote lengthy responses. And the best part was that they had initiated this all on their own. Farhana was thrilled to discover that her students were applying their learning in the most creative and engaging ways, and all voluntarily.

Digital tools allow students the flexibility to consolidate their learning in creative ways. They are able to apply their learning to things that are personally meaningful and engaging. When we give students the skills and the tools, we're often amazed what they do with them.

Critically Analyze

Along with the freedom that comes with the digital age comes the responsibility to critically analyze the information we encounter. When we begin to understand how things like wikis work, we realize that anyone, anywhere, can add to, delete, or change the information on such websites. Students need to be taught to examine information with a critical eye. They need to consider the source of the information, and the information itself, to determine if it is reliable and accurate. Too often, children believe that just because something is written, it must be true. In early years, they begin to question: "Is this in real life?" As early readers, youngsters need to decipher the difference between fiction and nonfiction. When they get older, these lines seem to get slightly blurry. Something may be presented as nonfiction but be filled with inaccuracies. Some information can include bias and distort the reality of a true event. Learning the difference between fiction and nonfiction is easy. Learning to critically analyze information is much harder.

See Digital Task Card: Fiction Facts on page 29.

Keep It Real

In a Grade 8 class, students learned to read historical fiction with a critical eye. They used nonfiction resources and information available on the Internet to evaluate the accuracy of the information contained in the text. Students compared the setting to real cities, towns, and countries. They read biographies of important historical figures and began to develop an understanding of the differences between how they were portrayed in the story and the factual information. They read first-hand accounts of historical events and evaluated the ways in which these same events were dramatized in the novels they were reading. These youngsters began to see the books they were reading in a new light. They understood the relevance of the time and history in which the books take place. They looked for inaccuracies, conflicts, or biases. These youngsters were thoughtful readers, and used all their resources to understand the context of the book. They worked at sifting through the novel to separate the fact from fiction. This was by no means an easy task, but they were armed with enough information to critically analyze of the content of the novels.

Digital Tools for Linking the Literacies

Digital literacy is the ability to access, understand, evaluate, and create information using digital tools. Students who are digitally literate are able to connect to the world, communicate effectively, apply their learning in creative ways, collaborate with others, consolidate their learning, and critically analyze the information they encounter.

"When my teacher allows us to use technology, it makes me feel like he really understands the way I learn, and it makes learning fun."

—Sara (Grade 5)

How can we intentionally link this new form of literacy into our existing literacies? What is the relationship between digital literacy and reading, writing, listening, and speaking? According to David Booth (2008), "Technology does not necessarily improve the acquisition of literacy. It requires carefully crafted learning programs focused on creating dynamic opportunities for interpreting, manipulating and creating ideas in the classroom." Can students be digitally literate without these other literacies? Obviously not. The digital world is text-driven and students need more than ever to be able to read, respond, and analyze information effectively and efficiently. Students need to understand the basic rules of communication (listening and speaking) to engage in purposeful interactions with other learners. Through this interaction of the literacies, we can strengthen not only students' digital skills, but their other literacies as well.

Wikis

What Is a Wiki?
A wiki is a simple tool that creates a document that can be accessed and edited by many users.

"Whenever we work together on a wiki, I can't wait to get back to it to see how it's changed."

—David (Grade 3)

A wiki can be used for any collaborative learning project. Teachers can create a wiki where students can add, change, or edit the information. When a user accesses a wiki, they have the option of reading, editing, or saving the document. This simple tool allows students to communicate with each other and work together.

See Digital Task Card: Class Newspaper on page 30.

Keep It Real

Teachers can use wikis as a forum for students to engage in shared writing projects. In a Grade 6 classroom, the students used a wiki as a way of creating a class newspaper. Every month, students accessed the wiki and signed up for the subject (or article) they were going to write. The newspaper also needed an editor and photographer. Throughout the month, students entered the wiki and completed their contributions. Finally, the editor read through all of the submitted articles, making any necessary changes. Once the newsletter was complete, the editor submitted the newspaper to the publisher (the teacher), who was able to print the newspaper for sharing with the parents.

Another group of Grade 4 students used their wiki as a literacy work station. The teacher started a number of different wikis, each with an exciting story beginning (see Digital Task Cards on pages 31, 32, 33). The students were able to access a wiki, read what had been written thus far, and continue the story. The students were excited to read the ideas of their classmates and add to the plot. Students thought of this simple writing activity as a writing game. They were anxious to return to the wiki to discover what happened next and the way in which the story had been changed, and they were eager to contribute more.

See Digital Task Cards: Story That Never Ends on pages 31, 32, 33.

Blogs

What Is a Blog?

A blog is a forum where one user can initiate a discussion topic and other users can post replies.

www.blogster.com
www.weblogg-ed.com

Keep It Real

Students in a Grade 4 class used a blog as a way of communicating about books with their teacher. The teacher gave the students a number of prompts and allowed the youngsters to respond through the use of a blog. The students were able to select books and a prompt to guide their response. Through this medium, the teacher was able to communicate with her students about their books, assess their understanding, and guide their learning.

Students in Grade 7 posted their writing on a blog and invited their peers to provide feedback. These students shared their writing with each other and used the feedback of their peers to improve their work and set goals for themselves. The teacher had spent time introducing her students to the concept of descriptive feedback. The students enjoyed the opportunity to share their writing with an audience of their peers and also relished the chance to read the writing of others. Through this process, the students' writing significantly improved and they developed a community of learners.

See Digital Task Card: Online Reading Response Journal on page 34.

See Digital Task Card: Writing Forum on page 35.

Blogs are a way for students to share their ideas and respond to the ideas of others. Blogs can be used to support students' reading, writing, and communication skills in a variety of ways.

Chatrooms

What Is a Chatroom?

A chatroom is an online space where users can engage in a conversation.

See Digital Task Card: Book Club Discussion on page 36.

See Digital Task Card: Math Chat on page 37.

> ## Keep It Real
>
> A group of Grade 5 students used their chatroom as a vehicle for their literature circle discussions. They moved their conversation about their books into the virtual world. These youngsters engaged in complex conversations, asked questions, and responded using evidence from their books to support their thinking. In this online book club, students discussed new vocabulary, made predictions, and inferred the intentions and feelings of the characters. They debated the importance of significant events and shared their connections to the text. In this chat, students were able to share their thinking, not only with students in their class, but also with the students of two other classes in neighboring schools. The three teachers collaborated to develop an online environment where students could meet others who were reading the same books and challenge each other with the depth of their thought. By broadening their circle of friends, students were able to add more voices to the rich discussion.
>
> Students in a Grade 6 class used a chat as a venue for discussing their math work. These students worked together, asking questions and sharing possible solutions to challenging math problems. With this form of communication, they were challenged to find the words to explain their thinking. They stretched the limits of their mathematical vocabulary and reasoning skills. As they engaged in these rich online conversations, they discovered the importance of explaining their thoughts, articulating their reasoning, and questioning the accuracy of others.

Chats take place in real time in an online environment. Student are able to enter a virtual room and join in a conversation. At first, it's a little tricky for students to understand the seemly random bits of dialogue. They may need some practice with chat etiquette. Often, there may be many conversations occurring simultaneously and it's important to know who you're chatting with. When chatting in an online environment, students should never use their real names, and definitely never include their last names.

Digital Stories

What Is a Digital Story?

A digital story is a series of images that is combined with either written or oral text to convey a message.

Digital stories are electronic picture books. Students are able to use a collection of images to tell a story. They can use a variety of sources to collect and compile the images. They can take pictures with a digital camera, they can draw and scan pictures using a simple scanner, or they can download images from the Internet that are suitable for use (see information in Chapter 3 about Creative Commons and copyright concerns). There are many simple photo applications that allow students to put their images into a logical sequence and add text, music, and even their own voice.

Digital cameras allow students the creative license to represent their ideas in a visual creative manner. With a digital camera, students are able to capture their world. Imagine the power of students capturing their authentic experiences in images, and using this as the basis for their writing.

Teachers will often select an image that is intended to motivate students' creative inspiration—and sometimes that works. But think of the power of providing students with the opportunity to capture an image that tells their own story. Students have stories to tell, and often it's not the stories we expect from them. Digital cameras are simple, relatively inexpensive tools that students can use to capture images that inspire them. Students can use these images as a catalyst for their writing.

See Digital Task Card: Forces in Sport on page 38.

Keep It Real

In a Grade 3 class, students used a simple digital story application to create a culminating task for a science unit on forces and movement. During the winter Olympics, they found images of the various sporting events that demonstrated the different forces at work (friction, gravity, etc). By assembling the images, and adding music, text, and their own voices, they succeeded in creating digital stories showing the wide range of forces at work

Teacher Websites

What Is a Website?

A website is an online space where different users can access and respond to information.

Many teachers are creating their own websites. This allows their students the freedom to access the Internet under the guidance of the teacher. Teachers are able to create websites and control the content of the site; their students are able to access specific information. Within a website, a teacher might include links to sites the students can visit, provide students with important information, and provide ways for students to respond. A teacher website is usually a secure online space that only students with a password are able to access. Typically, teachers who use websites are able to track the users on the site and monitor the ways in which they use it.

Teachers might choose to imbed other digital tools within their websites because of the simplicity of accessibility and the ease with which they can monitor their students. In this way, students are able to research information within the parameters set by the teacher. The risk of students surfing inappropriate sites is greatly reduced. Some teacher websites include a chatroom where students are able to connect and communicate with their peers, blogs where students can post and respond to information, wikis where students can collaborate on different projects, and journals where teachers and students can communicate privately with each other. Teachers can also post assignments that require students to upload a project. This can be anything from a presentation file or a digital story to a simple word document. Having all of your students work in a central loca-

"When I use digital games to help me learn, they are more fun, fast, and I know right away if I'm right or wrong"

—Matthew (Grade 2)

tion is highly beneficial, not only for the ease of access, but also because it allows many assignments to be paperless.

Teacher websites are perfect locations for students to post work and to respond to the work of others. Using blogs, students can share a piece of writing, recommend a book, or voice an opinion on a hot topic. Teachers can use a chatroom as a venue for a discussion about a book, a forum for conversations about science experiments, or any other form of dialogue you can imagine. The best feature of chatrooms imbedded in teacher websites is the fact that all conversations are archived; i.e., we have access to students' conversations at a later date. This allows us insight into their learning, thinking, and communicating. Also, when students use a teacher-created chatroom, the risk of cyberbullying is reduced, because the students are well aware of the fact that the teacher has access to all conversations. The convenience of linking all of the digital tools in one central location is the biggest advantage of a teacher website. The possibilities created with a website are limitless. It can be as simple or as complex as we choose.

Linking the Literacies

There are so many digital tools and countless applications for them. As teachers we need to explore the ways in which we can use these tools to engage our learners. We can provide authentic opportunities for them to apply their skills. When we start to weave the new literacies into the old literacies, we discover that students who are digitally literate rely on their other literacies. We can use digital tools as a way of strengthening students' writing. They can communicate about their reading, they can collaborate with others, they can use feedback from their peers as a way of setting goals for themselves as learners. With digital learning, they can connect to the world, consolidate their learning, and learn to critically analyze the information they encounter. Digital literacy is simply an extension of the other literacies.

Reading Connection

Tech Tool: Digital Mixing
What is a digital mixing application?
A digital mixing application allows users to combine tracks of music, sound effects, and audio recordings.

Digital Task Card: Book Soundtrack

Use a digital mixing tool to create a soundtrack for a book you are currently reading.

Create an audio soundtrack for a specific scene in the book.

Think about the mood of a particular event in the book. If it was part of a movie, what would the music sound like? Would it be fast or slow? Would it be happy, sad, or suspenseful? How can you use special effects and voice-overs to add to the interest of the piece?

Once you've finished the soundtrack, write a brief description of the events that are taking place during the scene.

Share your soundtrack with your classmates. If you've done a good job, they'll be able to visualize the book coming to life.

Pembroke Publishers. © 2010 *Keepin' It Real* by Lisa Donohue. ISBN 978-1-55138-260-9

Tech Tool: Search Engine
What is a search engine?
A search engine is a tool on the Internet that allows users to search for specific information.

Digital Task Card: Fiction Facts

After reading a historical fiction novel, use the Internet to do some research about the real-life events that took place during the book.

You may have read a book about a particular time in history (e.g., World War I, the Holocaust, medieval times, etc.); a historical figure (e.g., Martin Luther King Jr., Neil Armstrong, etc.,); a place in the world (e.g., ancient Rome, Pakistan, Africa, etc.); or a historical event (e.g., breaking down of the Berlin Wall, the abolition of slavery, the attack on the World Trade Center).

Use the Internet to find out as much information as possible on the subject matter of the book. You might look for actual pictures, maps, biographies, or personal accounts of incidents. Compare this to the information you have read in the book:

- How does it help you?

- Are there things that are different?

- Why do you think the author presented the information in the way that he/she did?

- Did you find any inaccuracies? Did that change your opinion of the book?

- What was the most important thing you learned that gave you more insight into the novel?

Pembroke Publishers. © 2010 *Keepin' It Real* by Lisa Donohue. ISBN 978-1-55138-260-9

Writing Connection

Tech Tool: Wiki
What is a wiki?
A wiki is a document that can be accessed and edited by many users.

Digital Task Card: Class Newspaper

Use a wiki to create a class newspaper.

Create a list of the articles that need to be included in the class newspaper: e.g., Science Scoop, Math Mania, Special Events Calendar, etc. Ask your classmates to sign up for the articles they plan on writing. The newspaper will also need an editor-in-chief.

Your peers can write different articles and then copy them into the wiki. Once all of the articles have been entered into the wiki, the editor can check the different articles to make sure that they all work well together.

You can either print the newspaper to share with others, or invite "subscribers" to read it electronically.

Pembroke Publishers. © 2010 *Keepin' It Real* by Lisa Donohue. ISBN 978-1-55138-260-9

Writing Connection

Tech Tool: Wiki
What is a wiki?
A wiki is a document that can be accessed and edited by many users.

Digital Task Card: Story That Never Ends #1

Use a wiki to create a "story that never ends."

You could use the following story starter, or one of your own, to begin a story. Continue the story by adding characters and exciting twists and turns to the plot. Save the story once you've added as much as you can. Encourage your friends to visit the wiki and add their ideas to the story. It is exciting to work with your friends on a writing project like this… you never know how it will end.

> The woods seemed unusually brighter. Often, I'd entered the woods during the day, and it seemed to be cloaked in darkness. However, today was different. There was a strange brightness coming from the forest floor itself. No creatures were visible. There was a faint humming noise coming from the carpet of moss. The breeze that often caused the massive oaks to sway and groan was completely absent today.
>
> I slowed my pace almost to a halt. My eyes needed time to adjust to the brightness that glowed around me. My feet seemed to be surrounded by a pulsing light. I sucked in my breath, I shielded my eyes, my mouth was agape in wonder. Never in my life had I seen the forest so alive and bright.
>
> Suddenly, from the corner of my eye, I noticed something lurking behind the shadows of one of the giant tree trunks. I turned quickly to see what was there, but the mysterious shadow had vanished, leaving a trail of glowing slime…

Pembroke Publishers. © 2010 *Keepin' It Real* by Lisa Donohue. ISBN 978-1-55138-260-9

Writing Connection

Tech Tool: Wiki
What is a wiki?
A wiki is a document that can be accessed and edited by many users.

Digital Task Card: Story That Never Ends #2

Use a wiki to create a "story that never ends."

You could use the following story starter, or one of your own, to begin a story. Continue the story by adding characters and exciting twists and turns to the plot. Save the story once you've added as much as you can. Encourage your friends to visit the wiki and add their ideas to the story. It is exciting to work with your friends on a writing project like this… you never know how it will end.

> The Fairy World was filled with magical things. Things that humans would never understand. There were spells, magical potions, and places that for generations had been hidden from human eyes.

> But today was different. The human child seemed to have powers that extended into the Fairy World. He heard the Fairy Song and answered its call. No human had ever before been able to hear the fairies—this would change their world forever.

> "Who are you?" he asked. "Where did you all come from?"

> The Fairies slowly emerged from their hiding places and began to introduce themselves.

Pembroke Publishers. © 2010 *Keepin' It Real* by Lisa Donohue. ISBN 978-1-55138-260-9

Writing Connection

Tech Tool: Wiki
What is a wiki?
A wiki is a document that can be accessed and edited by many users.

Digital Task Card: Story That Never Ends #3

Use a wiki to create a "story that never ends."

You could use the following story starter, or one of your own, to begin a story. Continue the story by adding characters and exciting twists and turns to the plot. Save the story once you've added as much as you can. Encourage your friends to visit the wiki and add their ideas to the story. It is exciting to work with your friends on a writing project like this… you never know how it will end.

> I walked into the mansion. I was taken aback by the size and grandeur of the room in which I stood. My footsteps echoed in the great hall, filling the huge room with the sound of my steps.
>
> "Hello?" I called. I waited breathlessly for a response, but none came. I felt my pulse quicken as my heart beat a little faster.
>
> The cold air of the large room seemed to fill my lungs and cool my body. I felt myself uncontrollably shiver—either out of fear or because of the sudden cold that seemed to surround me.
>
> "Hello?" I called again. My voice seemed to call back to me, but no response could be heard.
>
> I stood still, listening, straining my ears for any sound to indicate that I was not alone. I was certain that I could hear the faint sound of footsteps on the ancient wooden floor just above my head.

Pembroke Publishers. © 2010 *Keepin' It Real* by Lisa Donohue. ISBN 978-1-55138-260-9

Tech Tool: Blog
What is a blog?
A blog is a forum where one user can start a discussion and the other users can post replies.

Digital Task Card: Online Reading Response Journal

Use a blog as an online reading response journal. Here are some suggestions for entries:

- Write at least one paragraph describing one of the characters in the book you are currently reading. Choose a character that you can connect with. How is this character like you? Remember to include lots of details and evidence from the book to support your thinking.

- Write at least one paragraph describing something that you were able to clearly visualize in the book you are reading. Remember to include sensory words to describe what it looked like, felt like, sounded like, etc. Please include a direct quote from the book that supports your ideas. Remember to include the page number too.

- Write at least one paragraph describing a prediction that you made that actually happened in the book. Explain what you initially predicted and why you thought it would happen. Then tell what actually happened in the book. Don't you feel smart for getting it right?

- Can you use words like "visualize," "question," "predict," and "connect" to explain some of the ideas you're having while you're reading? Write at least one paragraph describing the reading strategies you're using to help you to understand the book you are currently reading.

- Write three paragraphs that summarize the main ideas of the book you are currently reading. Try to use sequencing words like "first," "then," and "finally." Remember to include the information that you think is the MOST IMPORTANT—this is not a place for lots of details, although evidence would be lovely!

Encourage your friends to read your blog and comment on your work.

Pembroke Publishers. © 2010 *Keepin' It Real* by Lisa Donohue. ISBN 978-1-55138-260-9

Writing Connection

Tech Tool: Blog
What is a blog?
A blog is a forum where one user can start a discussion and the other users can post replies.

Digital Task Card: Writing Forum

Use a blog as a forum for sharing your writing with other students and providing feedback to them.

With your teacher, agree on the success criteria for a piece of writing. These are the targets for your work. They describe the elements you need to include in your writing.

Success criteria are the targets for a piece of writing. For example, the success criteria for a narrative might include the following:

- The story contains characters, a setting, and a plot with a beginning, middle, and ending.

- The story includes an exciting problem with a creative resolution.

- The story includes correct spelling, grammar, and punctuation.

- The story includes connections to the writer's prior knowledge and experiences.

Post a piece of your writing on your blog, and invite your peers to provide you with feedback. Make sure that they are familiar with the success criteria. Encourage your classmates to include comments about the things you did well and to help you set goals for improving your work.

When you are sharing and responding to the work of others, it's important to always be respectful and kind. Try to phrase suggestions for improvement in positive ways: e.g., "Next time, think about adding more evidence to support your ideas."

Pembroke Publishers. © 2010 *Keepin' It Real* by Lisa Donohue. ISBN 978-1-55138-260-9

Reading Connection

Tech Tool: Chatroom
What is a chatroom?
A chatroom is an online space where users can have a conversation.

Digital Task Card: Book Club Discussion

Use the chatroom as a forum for book club discussion. You might choose to read the same book as other students, and pause throughout the book to have online conversations. The chatroom could be a virtual literature circle!

Find a group who would be interested in reading the same book and agree on dates for your online meetings. Decide how much of the book you plan on having read by each meeting. At the agreed-upon times, join your friends in cyberspace to share your thoughts on the book you are all reading. Here are some questions that might help guide your discussions:

- How do you think the main character felt when…?
- Would you have reacted in the same way?
- Do you agree with this character's decisions?
- What do you think he/she will do next?
- Why do you think this character is important to the story?
- What isn't the author telling us?
- How does this connect to things that happened earlier in the book?
- How do you think it will end?
- What do you like best/least about the book?
- Would you choose this character as a friend?

Pembroke Publishers. © 2010 *Keepin' It Real* by Lisa Donohue. ISBN 978-1-55138-260-9

Math Connection

Tech Tool: Chatroom
What is a chatroom?
A chatroom is an online space where users can have a conversation.

Digital Task Card: Math Chat

How can you use a chatroom to work with your classmates to solve a math problem?

Begin by posting a particularly challenging math problem (or your teacher may give you one to think about). Use the chatroom as a way of cooperating with each other to find a solution. You'll need to think about the different steps in solving the problem:

- What do you already know?

- What do you need to find out?

- How can you find your answer?

- How can you check to see if your work is correct?

You may be surprised to discover that your friends will find different ways to solve the same problem. If you used different methods, did you find the same answer? If not, how will you decide which is correct? Which solution did you find easier? Which method made more sense to you? If someone has suggested a solution that you don't understand, how can they clarify their thinking for you? How can you make sure that your thinking is clear for others?

Using words to communicate your thinking about mathematics is difficult—you'll get better at this with practice.

Pembroke Publishers. © 2010 *Keepin' It Real* by Lisa Donohue. ISBN 978-1-55138-260-9

Science Connection

Tech Tool: Digital Story
What is a digital story?
A digital story is a series of pictures that are combined with text to tell a story or share information.

Digital Task Card: Forces in Sport

Create a digital story that shows the way that different forces are at work in sports.

Search the Internet or use a digital camera to capture images that show which forces are most important in different sports. For example, you may want to show why friction is important in hockey, direction is important in baseball, and gravity is important in skiing. How many different forces can you find at work through sports?

Put the images together to form a digital story. Add text or your own voice to explain how each force is important to each sport. It's funny how hard forces have to *work*, when we *play*!

When you're finished, share your work with your friends.

Pembroke Publishers. © 2010 *Keepin' It Real* by Lisa Donohue. ISBN 978-1-55138-260-9

CHAPTER THREE

Media Literacy

"The illiterate of the 21st century will not be those who cannot read and write, but those who cannot learn, unlearn, and relearn."
—Alvin Toffler

For a Limited Time Only

We've all been caught by an advertising gimmick at some point. If it hasn't happened to you, either you're smarter than the rest of us, or—keep a look out—it's probably going to happen very soon. We've seen the infomercials, packed with testimonials and demonstrations, for products that seem like the simple fix, the smartest device, or the best solution. Since we've all been caught at one time or another, we tend to look at these promotional strategies with a critical eye. We look for the catch in the too-good-to-be-true scenario, we look for the small print in the free-trial-offer contract, and we scrutinize the details of the magazine advertisements.

"My little brother always wants everything he sees on commercials. I try to explain to him that advertising is sometimes biased—but I guess he just doesn't get that yet."
—Kirane (Grade 5)

If you have children of your own, you realize that this is a lifelong lesson that everyone needs to learn. My children always want the latest "but-it-said-so-on-the-commercial" product, and beg to eat at the local fast food restaurant because of some promotional toy they have "for a limited time only." Learning how to analyze and evaluate messages that are presented in the media is very difficult—an advanced skill, even for the smartest among us. That's because the people who market these products to us are highly-intelligent, well-paid, socially-aware executives. They are very conscious of their target audience. They know how to appeal to our senses, our emotions, our desires, and our insecurities. There is a good reason why they are so effective in convincing us to purchase a specific product. They are masters in media literacy.

In order for students to become more media literate, they need to view, analyze, and create a wide range of media forms. Media texts include advertisements, music, magazines, commercials, newspapers, images, websites, and movies. This is far from an exhaustive list because, in reality, media encompass anything that is created with the intention of communicating a message to an audience:

These texts abound in our electronic information age, and the messages they convey, both overt and implied, can have a significant influence on students' lives. For this reason critical thinking as it applies to media products and messages assumes a special significance. Understanding how media texts are constructed and why they are produced enables students to respond to them intelligently and responsibly. Students must be able to differentiate between fact and opinion; evaluate the credibility of sources; recognize bias; be attuned to discriminatory portrayals of individuals and groups… (*The Ontario Curriculum Grades 1–8: Language*)

www.media-awareness.ca/english/ teachers/media_literacy/what_is_ media_literacy.cfm

Media literacy is the ability to analyze, evaluate, and create messages using a variety of media forms. Media texts use words, graphics, images, and sounds. We are surrounded by numerous media messages from the minute we wake up in the morning and eat our cereal to the minute we go to bed at night. We have learned to be critical of the messages we encounter. We think about the source of the message, we look for biases, and we think critically about the information we encounter.

Youngsters need guidance to develop their awareness of the realities of media messages. They need to realize that sometimes there is more to a message than initially perceived. It's not that we want our children to become distrusting, sceptical pessimists. But we do want them to realize that most media messages have many layers. We want them to learn how to develop a deeper understanding of the way media messages are used to convey information, convince others, and change our actions or ideas.

Not all media messages are negative. In fact, many media messages are intended to motivate, support, encourage, and strengthen others. Consider anti-bullying campaigns, drug awareness campaigns, campaigns that promote positive self-image or inclusion of students with physical, social, or developmental challenges. Media messages serve to reduce discrimination and raise awareness for important causes like child-abuse or child poverty. These messages convey important information and challenge us to rethink, re-evaluate, and react.

How can we encourage our students to think more critically about what they hear, see, and read? In order to understand the way media messages work, they need to have the opportunity to take apart media works and put together media works. They need to think about the purpose of the piece, the message it is intended to convey, and the audience it targets. When students have the opportunity to create their own media texts, they start to think about the best way to share their message.

"I always see things on the TV and I say to myself, 'that can't be true.'"
—Cristina (Grade 4)

Students may be tasked with creating a public service announcement for a cause they believe in, an advertisement for a product they love, a piece of music for a book, a poster, a news article, a comic strip or photograph—the possibilities are endless. What mood, image, or impression are they trying to create? Students have many passions and strong opinions. If we can find a way for them to share things they are passionate about, they will be more able to convince others to share their passion.

Digital Tools for Creating Media Texts

There are many digital tools that can help students to create their own media texts. Student can use these tools to create messages in the form of podcasts, glogs, music, movies, comic strips, images, public service announcements, and many other creative applications.

Glogs

What Is a Glog?

www.glogster.com

A glog is a graphic blog. It allows users to layer images, text, video clips, and audio clips.

Glogs can be used to share messages by combining multiple forms of media into one presentation format. Users are able to add digital pictures, insert text, and insert audio clips with the greatest of ease. They are able to share their work and comment on glogs posted by others. Students can use glogs to create powerful media messages.

See Digital Task Card: Promoting Positive Self-Image on page 47.

Keep It Real

In a Grade 8 class, students used a series of glogs to promote positive self-image. They created numerous glogs that explored and found alternatives to the traditional view of beauty, friendship, athleticism, and talent. Students challenged each other to find appreciation in the unusual, the different, and the unique. They included pictures, poems, and audio clips. As the students started to post and share their glogs, they were surprised to discover how different each of their messages were. Students enjoyed sharing their glogs with others, but especially enjoyed responding to the work of their peers. They commented on the new and diverse ways they were challenged to view beauty and to think about friendship, respect, and abilities. The students broadened their discussion to include social issues like racism, discrimination, and bullying. The graphic nature of the original glogs let students post images and share their messages in a way that allowed greater discussion and depth of thought. Because students were able to respond to the work of their peers, the avenues of dialogue were opened. These students critically examined the social pressures that are put on them, thought about decisions they make, analyzed the source of their biases, and re-evaluated their values. Think of the literacies at work in such a simple task. Students are reading, writing, and responding. But better yet, students are creating, analyzing, evaluating, and thinking. What a powerful source for dialogue!

Podcasts

What Is a Podcast?

A podcast is a series of digital audio or video recordings.

Podcasts allow users to combine different forms of media in order to share a message with others. Podcasts can be as simple as an audio recording of a student's voice, or as complex as a commercial filled with video images, digital pictures, sound effects, and voice-overs.

"When I listened to David's podcast I really thought to myself: 'that must be a really great book', and I wanted to read it too,"
—Amber (Grade 3)

See Digital Task Card: Breaking News Broadcast on page 48.

Keep It Real

In a Grade 3 class, students created podcasts that were breaking news broadcasts. These 30- to 40-second presentations described the climax of a book. Students assumed the role of news anchors and summarized the problem of the story. Some students chose to include interviews with characters from the book, and some chose to report live from the scene. Either way, the students creatively integrated sound effects, special music, and their own voices in order to share their reading in a very exciting and engaging way. They were eager to listen to the podcasts of their peers and to respond in some way. The students were not only inspired by the use of the media tools, but were also engaged in the books they were reading, and eager to read the books their friends summarized.

Comic Creators

What Are Comic Creators?

See www.bitstrips.com and comic strip on page 15.

Comic creators are applications that allow users to generate comic strips. Users select images from a clipart gallery, add text in the form of speech bubbles or captions, and share their comic strips with others.

Comic creators can be used to create short comic messages that share information in a humorous way. Teachers are able to create a "class" on the site. Using this feature, they can ensure that they have opportunity to view all comic strips before they are shared with their peers. This eliminates the risk of the tool being used in inappropriate ways.

See Digital Task Card: Comic Creation on page 49.

Keep It Real

Students in a Grade 4 class used a comic creator to create comics that showed the importance of using technology in their schools and home. They were able to create simple comics that expressed how they felt about computers. They loved the simplicity and graphic nature of the tool. Students enjoyed responding to the comics of their peers.

Public Service Announcements

What is a Public Service Announcement (PSA)?

A public service announcement, or PSA, is a commercial that is intended to raise public awareness or change attitudes about a specific issue.

Public service announcements can be created using any number of media tools. Students could include digital photos, music, text, and audio or video clips. Through a PSA, students are challenged to find creative strategies to reach their target audience. They need to share a clear message in a way that would be convincing to others to change their attitude or behavior.

See Digital Task Card: Inclusion
Social Story on page 50.

Keep It Real

In a Grade 5 class, students used a simple digital photo application to create PSAs to promote inclusion of students with learning challenges. They researched different learning disabilities and compiled important facts. Students worked in small groups to role-play and photograph different scenarios around their school. They imported the images and sequenced them in the way that best told their "story." They inserted text, audio voice-overs, and background music to strengthen their message. These PSAs helped the students to develop a greater understanding of their peers and to share the important message that all students are to be respected, valued, and included.

<control> C, <control> V, <control> ME

Because the digital world is so accessible, it has become commonplace for students to decorate their work with Internet images, to cut and paste chunks of text, and to download and upload songs by the thousands. In this world of copy and paste, it is important to recognize that not everything can be legally used. Students have begun to think that any image, song, or text found on the Internet is free-gain. Plagiarism is rampant and copyright infringement is a serious concern. Copyright applies to all text, images, music, and other media found on the Internet.

www.creativecommons.ca
www.creativecommons.org

Creative Commons is an organization that allows creators to license their work and share it with others. Creative Commons licenses are free and can be applied to any work. They dictate how people may use, repurpose, or remix the work of creators. When students are accessing things on the Internet, it is important to teach them that not everything can be used creatively. Consider introducing students to the rules of copyright early and developing an understanding of right and wrong in the digital world.

Web 2.0 Tools

Throughout this book, I have tried to reference digital tools in general rather than naming specific software titles. This is because there are numerous tools that perform similar functions and, in the rapidly changing digital world, new sites and applications are appearing on a daily basis. Where resources are unique (at the time of writing, anyway), I use the specific names, including Prezi, VoiceThreads, and Twitter. Most Web 2.0 tools are free to download and use.

At the time I wrote this book, there were over 3,400 different Web 2.0 tools. To think that one could be an expert in all of these areas is not only unrealistic, but also impractical. One of the nice things about Web 2.0 tools is that they are all quite user-friendly. This allows for easy exploration and experimentation.

Web 2.0 tools allow us to use the programs, store our information online, and access our work from any Internet connection. Students can save their work and share it with anyone. Often with traditional software, I would find that my students saved their work, only to discover that they did not have the necessary program on their home computer to open the file. With Web 2.0 tools, this issue has been resolved. By logging on to the tool online, they are able to upload, edit, save, and share their work. This allows students easier access to a greater variety of tools. Many of these Web 2.0 tools have valuable classroom applications. Here are just a few:

Prezi

What Is a Prezi?

www.prezi.com

Prezi is a non-linear presentation format. It allows users to add images and text in indefinite space.

With Prezi, users create a "map" of the information they wish to share. They navigate through the map by creating a path through their images and texts. With Prezi, they can zoom into and out of the space, and can hide images or text within other things.

See Digital Task Card: Virtual Tour of the Solar System on page 51.

> ## Keep It Real
>
> Students in a Grade 6 class used the unique features of a Prezi to create a virtual tour of the solar system. They compiled information on each of the planets, the sun, and various other features of the solar system: e.g., asteroid belt, Jupiter's Red Spot, the rings of Saturn, etc. As the students added images to the Prezi, they were able to navigate through the different celestial bodies. They zoomed close to the sun, surfed on the rings of Saturn, and melted into Mercury. The students were completely engaged, learning about space and the planets, and presenting it all in such a creative and unique way.

VoiceThreads

What Is VoiceThreads?

www.voicethread.com

VoiceThreads is an online collaborative conversation tool.

VoiceThreads is a multimedia tool that allows users to respond to slideshows in a number of ways (audio, text, or video). Users can view an image and join in the conversation. They can post a response to an ongoing dialogue by recording an audio response (with a cell phone or computer), a written response (through texting or a computer), or a video response.

See Digital Task Card: Issues Forum on page 52.

> ## Keep It Real
>
> A Grade 6 class used VoiceThreads as a medium to discuss the catastrophic 2010 oil spill in the Gulf of Mexico. Their teacher posted an image showing the oil spilling into the ocean and students used VoiceThreads as a forum to comment. They posted audio comments, text comments, and video responses. They gathered research about the dangers to the wildlife in the surrounding areas, they shared their scientific discoveries about the realities of the event, and they posted numerous suggestions for resolving the problem. The students used this forum as way of expressing their grave concerns for the environment and the future of the oceans. They proposed actions that should be taken to rectify the problem as well as suitable consequences for the people responsible. They were connected to the realities of world events and they were able to have their voice heard.

Tag Clouds

What Is a Tag Cloud?

www.wordle.net

A tag cloud is a graphic image created with words.

Tag cloud software uses any given text to create an image using the words. Users can copy and paste a selection of text into the tool and it will automatically create an image using those words.

In a classroom, teachers can use tag clouds as a way for students to reflect on their writing. It shows them when they are overusing a word or underrepresenting an idea. Finally, students can use them to celebrate their writing in fun, exciting ways. After all, they look really cool!

Online Book Clubs

What Are Online Book Clubs?

www.shelfari.com

Online book clubs, like Shelfari, are social networking sites for readers.

Users are able to create virtual bookshelves showing the books they have read. They can post comments, summaries, and recommendations about these books. Like any social networking site, users can create friend lists of people, in this case, those with whom they can share conversations about their books.

Evolution in Action

In Don Kemball's Grade 6 class, his students post summaries, share recommendations, and have conversations with their "reading buddies" in another school. They are able to use this new form of social networking to connect, collaborate, and communicate with other students. These students became eager to add to their bookshelves and began reading more voraciously than ever. They particularly enjoyed having the opportunity to engage in rich dialogues with other students about their books. Their real bookshelves expanded as a direct result of their virtual shelves.

Linking the Literacies

How does media literacy support students reading, writing, listening, and speaking? By creating a wide range of media presentations, students explore new forms of communicating. They recognize the importance of sharing their ideas in clear, concise ways. Students find ways to have their voices heard, and understand the importance of listening, analyzing, and evaluating the messages of others.

Writing

Two of the biggest influences on a writer are audience and authenticity. When writers write with an audience in mind, they consider the reader. They are aware of the conversation they are having with the reader and of the importance of deciding what information to include, what should be omitted, and the best way to find their voice through written words. Readers bring purpose to writing. Writing is intended to be used as a form of communication and, when we share our writing with others, it brings value to the work. Providing students with authentic writing experiences helps to increase engagement and motivation.

Students are more likely to find inspiration in authentic writing tasks about topics they are directly connected to and concerned about, than when writing just for the sake of writing. Authenticity means that students write for a real purpose: to share information, to persuade or convince others, to entertain, or to reflect. This authenticity allows students to see the importance of expressing themselves through the written word. They recognize the need to clearly articulate their ideas in order to communicate effectively.

Experiences with media literacy allow students these opportunities. When students create media texts, they are writing authentic pieces with a very clear audience in mind. They know who will read their work and so consider how best to share their information. Media texts encourage students to find their voice in creative, integrated ways. They can combine image, text, and sounds. They make decisions that directly influence the way in which their reader will interpret and respond to their message. Students think about the message they want a reader to get from their work. They think about the mood they wish to convey, and they think about the way they want their reader to react. These media literacies are a natural extension of writing. We want our writers to think about their readers. We want them to think about the ways in which they will read, react, and respond to their words. Media texts allow writers a greater opportunity to create authentic texts, share them with real audiences, and receive feedback about the effectiveness of their pieces through their readers' responses.

Reading

Effective readers use a wide range of strategies to interact with texts. They ask questions, determine importance, make inferences, and synthesize the information. These skills are more important than ever when reading media texts. Readers need to question the source of message and the accuracy of the information. They need to "read between the lines" and look for the hidden intent behind the piece. Finally, they need to compare and integrate the new information with their existing knowledge.

Students who are taught to be savvy readers when interacting with media texts are more able to detect bias and question the reliability of the information. Youngsters are taught from an early age that there are two distinct types of texts: fiction and nonfiction. Media texts sometimes blur those lines. Readers need to be critically aware of the information they are reading, and to think about the underlying message. We need to teach students these skills. Media texts are distinctly different from other texts and challenge our students to become more critical and analytical readers.

Listening and Speaking

Media texts allow for the integration of many different text forms. Students can include audio input, video input, visual information in the form of images, and written text. Through this array of shared information, they are challenged to listen carefully and speak clearly when interacting through media texts. Many digital tools allow students to add their voice with simple digital recording devices (through cell phones or direct input from the computer). As students listen to others and themselves, they discover the importance of being concise, clear, and articulate when they speak. They learn to use inflection as a way of strengthening the message they are trying to send. Through multimedia presentation formats, students learn to integrate all of the literacies. They must listen carefully, speak clearly, read critically, and write purposefully.

Tech Tool: Glog
What is a glog?
A glog is a graphic blog. It is a way of sharing images, text, audio and video clips with others.

Digital Task Card: Promoting Positive Self-Image

Create a glog that will promote positive self-image in young adolescents.

Think of a way you can challenge the traditional views of beauty, friendship, athleticism, and talent. How can you find ways of appreciating the unusual, different, and unique features in everyone?

Use images, text, and audio and video clips in your glog as a way of encouraging others to see themselves through a positive lens. Convince your viewers that different is special. How can you portray these differences as positive?

Save and share your glog with others. Encourage them to share their opinions with you. Use your glog as a forum to think about social pressures, decisions you are challenged with, and biases you have encountered in society.

Pembroke Publishers. © 2010 *Keepin' It Real* by Lisa Donohue. ISBN 978-1-55138-260-9

Tech Tool: Podcast
What is a podcast?
A podcast is a series of digital audio or video recordings.

Digital Task Card: Breaking News Broadcast

Create a podcast that sounds like a breaking news broadcast.

Select a book that you have recently read. Think of an exciting event in the book that could have made the evening news.

- Create a script for an interview with one or more of the characters. Ask your friends to play the parts of the characters and record their responses.

- You can pretend to be the news anchor and describe the important events in the book.

Once you've recorded your piece, add special effects and music jingles to begin and end your Breaking News Broadcast.

Share your podcast with your classmates. Invite them to comment on your work. Perhaps your podcast will inspire them to read the book.

Pembroke Publishers. © 2010 *Keepin' It Real* by Lisa Donohue. ISBN 978-1-55138-260-9

Writing Connection

Tech Tool: Comic Creator
What is a comic creator?
A comic creator is a tool that allows the user to employ a bank of graphic images to create comic strips.

Digital Task Card: Comic Creation

Create a glog that will promote positive self-image in young adolescents.

Create a comic strip that shows how you feel about learning new things at school. You can use humor—through words and body language—to help convey your ideas.

You might choose to create a comic strip that shows how you feel when you work on computers, complete science experiments, approach artistic tasks, work cooperatively with your peers, or are faced with a challenging math problem. You might include things you've learned in science, social studies, or another subject.

You'll need to be selective about the text you include. Try to express a point of view, to state your opinion, or to make a joke in a few short sentences.

Remember to always be respectful to your teachers and peers.

Pembroke Publishers. © 2010 *Keepin' It Real* by Lisa Donohue. ISBN 978-1-55138-260-9

Tech Tool: Digital Story
What is a digital story?
A digital story is a series of pictures that are combined with text to tell a story or share information.

Digital Task Card: Inclusion Social Story

Use a digital story to create a social story about how and why students with different exceptionalities should be included in our classrooms and games.

Use the Internet and nonfiction resources (books, magazines, texts, etc.) to find information about students with different exceptionalities. These may be physical challenges or learning disabilities.

Create a series of images that shows ways in which we can all be friends to students with exceptionalities.

- What do we need to know in order to support them better?

- How can we include others in our learning and our games?

Combine images with your research to create a digital story. Save and share your story with your classmates.

Pembroke Publishers. © 2010 *Keepin' It Real* by Lisa Donohue. ISBN 978-1-55138-260-9

Science Connection

Tech Tool: Prezi
What is a Prezi?
Prezi is an interactive presentation format. With a Prezi, you can create a project with infinite space; you can zoom into and out of images.

Digital Task Card: Virtual Tour of the Solar System

Use the Prezi presentation format to create a virtual tour of our solar system.

You can use images of each of the planets and the sun. Add pictures to the Prezi, and plan how you can navigate through our galaxy. Use each image as a place to record information about the celestial bodies found in space. You can zoom into the sun to find out more, surf the rings of Saturn, and bounce on the moon.

You'll need to place the images first and think about how you will organize your virtual tour. Once you've created the solar system, add some information about each item. Use the Internet or nonfiction books to research the different parts of our galaxy. Remember to respect copyright on images and information. You need to write your ideas using your own words.

Create a path that will zoom through the galaxy at the speed of light.

Save and share your Prezi with your friends.

Pembroke Publishers. © 2010 *Keepin' It Real* by Lisa Donohue. ISBN 978-1-55138-260-9

Social Studies Connection

Tech Tool: VoiceThread
What is a VoiceThread?
VoiceThreads is an online tool that allows users to have an ongoing conversation. Participants can respond with text, audio, or video entries.

Digital Task Card: Issues Forum

Use VoiceThreads to create a forum for a discussion about an important social, historical, or environmental issue.

The VoiceThread needs to start with one image that will invite others to join in the discussion. Choose an image that is clear and directly connects to the theme of the discussion. You can use an image that you've taken with a digital camera or one from the Internet. Make sure that you respect copyright rules when using Internet images.

Start the discussion thread with an audio, video, or text entry. Invite your classmates to join in the discussion and add their opinions to the conversation.

You can start a VoiceThread on any topic, but here are some suggestions to get you started:

- Who was the most influential person in history?
- What should be done about the pollution of our oceans, rivers, and lakes?
- How can we respond to natural disasters in other countries?
- What can we do in our community to make the world a better place?

Pembroke Publishers. © 2010 *Keepin' It Real* by Lisa Donohue. ISBN 978-1-55138-260-9

CHAPTER FOUR

Social Literacy

"The primary aim of education is not to enable students to do well in school, but instead to do well in the lives they lead outside of school."
—Elliot W. Eisner

Play Nicely, Share Your Toys, and Take Turns

www.socialliteracytoday.com

The earliest skills we learn are social ones. We teach our toddlers words like "please" and "thank you"; they say "bye-bye" and blow kisses. As they get a little older, they learn to take turns and share. We teach them the importance of using their words, instead of hitting or pushing, to express their feelings. We help them understand the feelings of others and we try to develop in them a sense of empathy for those around them. At first, children see themselves as the centre of the world but, as they grow, they begin to understand how the world works and how they fit into it. They learn to communicate with others; they learn to play cooperatively with their friends; they share their toys and use their words to solve their problems (most of the time, anyway). They learn the appropriate ways in which we interact with each other. Even at an early age, children can explain the rules of social interactions. They know what is acceptable behavior and that they need to adapt their behavior to suit different situations. These are social literacies.

Social literacy refers to one's ability to communicate, connect, and relate to those around in effective ways. When people are socially literate, they are able to engage in a variety of social interactions and adjust their behavior based on the context of the situation. They can understand messages that are conveyed both verbally and nonverbally. Social literacy allows people to "read" each other and express themselves.

Social literacy is also an understanding of the norms we use to interact with others. We understand that we need to treat others in a fair manner and with respect. We know that we need to listen and be heard. We are sensitive to the different backgrounds, religions, races, and beliefs of the people around us. Being socially literate means that we are thoughtful about the ways in which we interact with others and are aware of the power our words can have. Social literacy encompasses all forms of communication; from telephone conversations to locker-room conversations, and from text messages to complex essays. Through these forms of communication, we are sharing and interpreting information and ideas with the world around us.

Evolution in Action

Character expert Arthur Birenbaum believes that social literacy extends beyond the classroom, beyond the playground, and into the community. He weaves social literacy into the very culture of the school and community.

Arthur begins the process by working with a group of students aptly named the Character Council (as opposed to School Council). These students survey the students, the staff, and the parents in the community to determine the character attributes they value most. This extends beyond simplistic catch-phrases—initiative, optimism, respect, responsibility, honesty, integrity, etc. Instead, the students work together to define, not what these words mean, but instead what they look like, sound like, and feel like. The students define the *actions* not the *words*. Once the Character Council has received input from all groups that contribute to the school climate, they begin to assemble their statements into a touchstone. A touchstone is a code of behaviors that all students agree to, believe in, and are committed to developing in their school. The fact that the touchstone is student-developed ensures that it accurately represents their wants, needs, and beliefs; therefore, students have ownership in the process and the outcome. The touchstone is a common language that all students, teachers, and parents can use to communicate about behavior. When students act in a way that breaks the agreement, they are encouraged to examine the touchstone, and find a way to realign their behavior. These touch-stones are shared here with the permission of the school principals:

> At our school, we care for others and encourage everyone to do their best.
> The many different cultures and traditions of our community are accepted, respected and cherished.
> Everyone takes initiative to do positive things for ourselves, our friends and the world around us.
> We are kind to those in need of a friend; we are a light unto others.
> We are willing to be risk-takers…
> Having confidence in ourselves allows us to set goals to achieve success.
> We admit when mistakes happen and take responsibility for our choices.
> We are an eco-friendly school, caring about our planet.
> Everyone is free to play; no one is excluded.
> We never say never.
> (Kettle Lakes Public School)

> At our school, we take responsibility for our work, words, and actions.
> We put in our best efforts, enjoy our successes, and learn from our mistakes.
> We embrace each other's differences and care for each other's feelings.
> We think before we speak and use words that are appropriate for school.
> Our community is a safe community; a place where we treat people with kindness, respect, and dignity.
> No one is afraid at our school.
> We are free to succeed!
> (Richmond Rose Public School)

This shared understanding builds a sense of community and personal responsibility. Students recognize that they all play an important part in the culture of the school. The touchstone is present in every class and throughout the halls. But it is more than a visual presence in the school. It is the way in which students use it to guide, monitor, and redirect their actions that makes it a powerful tool. It is the basis for conflict resolution, the foundation for involvement in charitable actions, and the platform on which students learn to act and respond appropriately in social situations.

How does this social literacy connect to the other literacies? Students use the touchstone as a foundation for reading, writing, and responding. They also use a wide range of media texts to share and promote social literacies within the school and community. Students create posters, slideshows, podcasts, musical and dramatic presentations. They blog about world issues that connect to the touchtone. They write poetry, stories, journals, reflections—and the list goes on. The touchstone is a conscious awareness of social literacy in the school. It reminds students that they are a part of something bigger than their individual selves, and that they must act in a way that contributes to the culture of not only their school, but also their society. They are global citizens.

Global Awareness

With the world connected through a medium such as the World Wide Web, students are able to develop a sense of global awareness. Where do they fit in this big world? Students can become a part of the global community of learners and citizens. They are able to communicate with students in other schools, cities, or even countries. They can work collaboratively with people they would otherwise never have the opportunity to meet.

See Digital Task Card: Where You Live on page 63.

Keep It Real

Students in a Grade 4 class went on brief walk around their neighborhood and through a local wooded area. As they explored, they captured images of the plants, insects, animals, and animal tracks that they found. They discovered a swampy area teeming with life and a rotten tree filled with insects; they followed the path of a trail of ants and examined the tiny flowers covering the forest floor. They were equipped with digital cameras and were in teams of "observers." They were surprised to capture such a vast array of wildlife living in the surrounding habitats. Upon their return to the school, students used the pictures they had taken to find out more about the local plants and animals. They discovered that the unique green flower they found is indeed toxic; they realized that the wild berries are not edible; and they learned that the large bulges in the thick stalks of the weeds are the homes for the larva of an insect. They used the images to create a digital photo story, showing the life that exists in their surrounding habitats. They learned about producers, consumers, and decomposers. They were able to identify different plants, not because they read about them in a book, but because they were first seeing them in real life. They were intrigued and searched for answers to their questions.

Not only are students able to connect and communicate, but they are also able to actively bring about change. Young people are able to have their opinions heard, and to make a difference in the world in which they live. Through digital tools, there is an equal opportunity for every voice to be heard, every voice to be equal. Young people who are global citizens see the world as an interconnected place. They understand the significance of global events. With tools like video streaming and virtual field trips, students can view the world without ever leaving their classroom. With tools like blogs and wikis, they can share their voice with a large audience. Developing a sense of interconnectedness enables students to understand their global responsibility and citizenship.

Traditional Literacies as Social Literacies

Writing

When students are writing, they are using a broad number of social skills. They are thinking about the conversation they are creating with their reader. They are thinking about perspective and voice. They prioritize information, sequence details, and make connections to their background knowledge. Writers determine what information is important to state directly and what can be left for the reader to infer. Effective writers write for an audience. They know who will read the words they have written and think of the ways in which their writing will make someone respond. These are all socially-driven communication skills. Writers are communicating and connecting to those around them. Effective writers are able to write for a wide range of audiences and to adjust the form and content of their writing to suit the context of the situation. Writing is a social literacy. In order to communicate effectively, a writer must be effective in expressing his/her ideas in a way that allows others to read and interpret the words.

"Sometimes, my friends make even better suggestions than I could have ever thought of on my own."
—Amaria (Grade 7)

When we engage in face-to-face conversations, we have nonverbal cues that help us to interpret the speakers' intentions. A raised eyebrow might indicate a sarcastic comment, and we are alerted to the fact that the words may not match their meaning. A shrug of the shoulders can convey more meaning than the words spoken. Interpreting these subtleties of communication is a skill that we apply automatically. However, with writing, the reader has only the words on the page to interpret the author's intent. There are no visual cues to indicate the mood or intent of the writer. Thus, we need to teach our students to use their "voice" in their writing. By using voice, writers are able to add expression to their words and aid the reader in understanding the author's intent.

Reading

When we read, we are engaging in a dialogue with the author. We are reading the words, creating images in our mind, and predicting what is to come. Effective readers are not passive observers, but are constantly making meaning from the text. We infer and synthesize, we make connections to our own experiences, and we empathize with the characters in the story. By reading, we are connecting to others through text. They are communicating with us and we are responding.

"If I can share my ideas with others, it helps me to really understand myself as a learner."
—Julia (Grade 5)

The level of our engagement with a given text depends on how much we can relate to it. We understand the actions of characters in a book because we understand the nuances of social literacy. We are able to predict how someone might react or feel because we may have had a similar experience. We can visualize a specific setting because the author describes it in such a way that we are able to picture it clearly in our minds. Effective writers take this social interaction into account as they are writing. They are aware of their audience, and write in a way to hold their reader in an engaging "conversation."

Listening and Speaking

It seems like listening and speaking are the core of social literacies. Social literacy requires us to communicate effectively through listening and speaking. It means that we are able to listen to the words spoken and understand the message that is being conveyed. It also requires that we clearly articulate our own ideas and express them in a way that others can understand. The social norms of conversation require us to adjust the pace of our words, the tone of our voice, our gestures and body language, depending on the situation in which we are communicating. Likewise, we learn to listen, question, and interpret the information that other speakers are sharing with us.

Moving Into the Digital World

The Internet has brought the world into our homes and classrooms, and has provided us with a broader audience with which we can communicate. We can engage in face-to-face interactions or online communications that allow us to communicate with virtually anyone, anywhere. Social networking in the digital world has required us to become even more socially literate. Ironically, the biggest challenge that comes with broadening the circle of people with whom we communicate is that too often we lose sight of the fact that we are still communicating with real people in real places. We lose the human aspect of communication. Social literacy in the digital world requires a set of communication skills similar to those we use in the real world.

Netiquette

What is netiquette? Derived from the words "network" and "etiquette," netiquette refers to a set of guidelines that help people use good manners when working in cyberspace. Often, when students are communicating electronically, they lose touch with the reality that they are interacting with other people. Some of the nuances of face-to-face communication are lost. They can't use their facial expressions, tone of voice, or body language to help convey the message. Therefore, users need to be very careful of the words they choose to express themselves. Students need to be aware that their messages are taken literally and at face value; they need to be articulate and clear. When communicating with others online, they need to represent themselves in the best way possible—grammar and spelling do count! When your students are responding to the work of others, encourage them to make suggestions or ask questions instead of criticizing. Finally, students need to remember to treat each other with respect. They should never say anything online that they would not be comfortable saying in person.

Some teachers create netiquette norms with their students. A list of such rules might look like this:

"Literacy is bound up with our identity and our practices… who we are, and who we are allowed to be is shaped in part by the way we use literacy."
—Pahl and Rowsell (2005)

www.albion.com/netiquette/corerules.html

57

- Use proper words and sentences.
- Be respectful and considerate of others' work. Never criticize someone's work; instead provide feedback or suggestions that may help them improve.
- Before posting your work, make sure you have checked it carefully and it represents your best thinking. Check your work for spelling, grammar, and clarity of ideas.
- Always be polite and use appropriate language. Never post something that will humiliate, embarrass, threaten, or discriminate against someone.
- Tell your teacher if you encounter anything that makes you feel uncomfortable. Never respond to inappropriate posts.

"Everyone needs to have good manners when they're working with the computers. We need to be polite just like in real-life."

—Marcus (Grade 3)

Creating a Social Identity

Many youngsters use social networking sites as a way of keeping in touch with their friends. They share stories, post pictures, and update their status on a regular basis. Many adolescents consider this an extension of their face-to-face social network. Unfortunately, many of them are oblivious to the public nature of the forum. Students need to be aware that they are creating an online social identity. The things they post can be easily accessed by schools, potential employers, and other organizations. Students need to realize that, in this day of social literacies, the words they use and the image they convey matter. And that image can follow them for a very long time. They may feel that the information they post on these sites is personal and private; however, if they are using a public forum, they need to consider the ramifications.

Cyberbullying

The Journal of Adolescent Health (2007) found that more than 80% of adolescents owned at least one form of digital technology used for communicating with others, presenting information about themselves, and sharing media creations. While the digital world has many benefits, there are risks associated with being so intricately connected, including giving bullies access to a whole new medium for targeting others.

With the high prevalence of digital access, the best approach to reduce cyberbullying is education. Students need to understand the reality of both sides of bullying. Victims need to know what to do if they are being bullied, and perpetrators need to realize that they are not as anonymous as they may feel. While some students might feel powerful behind the keys of a computer, others can feel powerless. Neither is the truth. If a student ever feels bullied, threatened, intimidated, or belittled, he/she should immediately print a copy of the communication that made him/her feel this way. The student should in no way respond; instead he/she should share the information immediately with an adult. Police take cyberbullying very seriously and have the tools to trace the source of the message.

Teachers should work with students to develop netiquette norms for online communications. They should also help students identify risks they may encounter. Educating our students about the risks and realities of cyberbullying is our best line of defense.

Streetproofing for the 21st Century

When I was a child, I remember the day I was entrusted with a key to our home. It was a great honor to be finally old enough to be trusted with a set of keys. This honor came with a great deal of responsibility. I knew that I was never to let a stranger into the house, I should never admit to being home alone, and I was to inform my parents should I misplace the key. As a child, I clearly understood the dangers. I could see the risk of someone entering our home and I could imagine the potential dangers.

It was much easier to detect danger when it was staring me in the face. Now the risks are much more subtle. Through the use of technology, the world is never far away. And, for the most part, that's a good thing. However, there is the danger that children can encounter people with ulterior motives. Streetproofing our kids is an essential social skill.

Evolution in Action

Will Richardson, a strong advocator for digital learning, has said, "Kids are coming to the Web earlier and earlier, and it's obviously very important that we prepare them for life online." He encourages us to have ongoing dialogue with our students and their parents about what information they can share and what information should be kept private. He also explains the importance of teaching our students what to do, should they encounter inappropriate content on a site. Will stresses the importance of preparation, especially when it comes to working with our younger students. We should be familiar with the sites we are asking them to visit, they should be knowledgeable about the information they are permitted to share, and they should know what they need to do if they encounter anything inappropriate.

See Digital Task Card: Substance Abuse on page 65.

Keep It Real

In a Grade 6 class, students used Prezi to create presentations about the dangers of various illicit drugs. Each student collected information, images, and quotes about different substances. They assembled their research using a Prezi. In this way, students were able to use the images, quotes, and information as "talking points" when sharing their work with the class. They recognized the danger of these illicit drugs, and used this medium to raise awareness and discourage their peers from experimenting with drugs. Students loved the fact that they were able to create hidden elements in their presentation, to zoom in and out of their information, and to create original and unique media presentations. They recognized the importance of trying to convince their peers that their message is important. These students were able to create a message for a target audience with the intention of affecting the decisions they make.

Cyber-risks and Strategies

The following are some risks that children may encounter in cyberspace. We can't prevent them from encountering these things, but we can educate them about what to do should it happen to them.

Flaming

A negative, hostile, or insulting statement made by texting, e-mail, or instant message.

To prevent flaming:
- Do not respond.
- Save or print the message and share it with a trusted adult.

Phishing

An attempt to get private information by imitating a trusted source.

To protect yourself against phishing:
- Always know who you are communicating with.
- Never provide user names, passwords, or private information, such as last names, addresses, or phone numbers.

Grooming

The intentional establishment of a relationship between a predator and a child; the predator tries to befriend and create an emotional connection to the child with the intention of harming him or her.

To protect yourself from grooming:

- Always know who you're talking to online.
- Never give out personal information.
- Never post pictures of yourself.
- Never agree to meet someone you've met online.
- Tell an adult you trust if you feel uncomfortable with any online communication.

Cyberbullying

Repeated threats, put-downs, and attempts at intimidation that are intended to harm someone.

To protect against cyberbullying:

- Don't give out personal information on the Internet.
- Don't send messages when you're angry.
- Never open messages from someone you don't know.

To respond to cyberbullying:

- Print or save as much information as possible.
- Do not delete the threats.
- Inform the police and Internet provider.

Using Digital Tools to Support Social Literacy

Blogs

Blogs allow students to express their ideas, opinions, and thoughts. Students can use their written voice to share information with an authentic audience. Using blogs, students can capture their own ideas and feelings while connecting and communicating with others. According to Lisa Zawilinski (2009), blogs broaden the audience for student writing and thinking. A blog provides a space for collaborating outside the classroom, makes more room for discussion and problem-solving, and helps students learn how to communicate safely on the Internet. Mohr and Orr (2009) found that students who were extremely shy, after using blogs as a venue for responding to reading, were more able to express themselves, and that students began to foster more supportive relationships among each other. Blogging gave students an authentic audience for their writing, and they learned how to respond to each other in ways that strengthened, not only their reading and writing skills, but also their social literacy.

Wikis

The dynamic nature of a wiki requires social collaboration, as a number of writers work together to create, edit, and add to a shared document. Students need to agree on the ways in which they will cooperate in order to share and value everyone's input. When working together, students need to demonstrate respect for everyone's work. Working together on a shared writing project requires students to reason, negotiate, and cooperate with people they may not typically select to work with. According to Texas A&M University, Corpus Christi, "collaborative writing is a complex process that requires collaborators to negotiate social relationships of authority, power, responsibility, and conflict." (*Kairos 10.1*) The use of wikis can help to build a community of writers, helping everyone let their voice be heard and actively contribute to the conversation.

"Wikis help us to work as a team—even if we're not together."
—Serina (Grade 7)

Chatrooms

A chatroom is exactly that, an online conversation. When someone enters a chatroom, he/she needs to show many of the same social skills required when entering a crowded room of people. It would be rude to dominate a face-to-face conversation; likewise, it is not socially polite to dominate an online conversation. Would you enter a room and just jump into the conversation, or would you listen for a while first to discover what people were talking about? This is also important in chatroom netiquette. As with any dialogue, we need to listen and respond in appropriate ways. We need to keep pace with the conversation and add our thoughts when appropriate. We should not attempt to dominate or manipulate the conversation, or use language that would offend others. These are simple norms of social conversations—but they also apply in cyberspace.

Linking the Literacies

Mohr and Orr (2009) found that when students were connected to a larger audience, it had a tremendous effect on their reading and writing. The students were more motivated to share their ideas because they knew that classmates and teachers throughout the school were reading their work. When students can share their writing with a broader community of learners, they write more and write better. Ramaswami (2008) concluded that students who used an interactive online tool were able to better organize their thoughts, develop their ideas, synthesize their research, and apply the feedback of their classmates. Allowing students an authentic place to share their writing and respond to the writing of others not only strengthened their social literacy, but improved their reading and writing as well.

When students used a reader's notebook to respond to their reading, Mohr and Orr (2009) discovered that their responses were limited. This was the case because their only discussion partner was their teacher. However, when they moved to using blogs as a forum for responding to their reading, the conversation expanded and allowed for a variety of perspectives. Bringing more voices into the conversation allowed for a greater depth of thinking. Students were able to communicate, question, validate, and support the thinking of their peers. They wrote more because they knew that what they wrote mattered. They knew that they were engaging others in conversation. Students discovered that when they wrote interesting things, they received interesting responses. If they wanted to hook their audience, they needed to write exciting things. Their writing took on a sense of audience and voice.

Finally, Coiro (2009) concluded that students who participate actively in using digital tools are able not only to gain new knowledge from their reading, but also to create and share their knowledge with other members of the global community. These students begin to understand their responsibility as global citizens. They realize that they can support the learning of others and share their understandings with a broader audience.

Social literacy directly strengthens students' reading, writing, speaking, and listening. Students are able to use these other literacies to actively participate in the global learning community. We need to ensure that students have the opportunity and skills needed to engage in this new literacy.

"When I know that my friends will read and comment on my writing it motivates me to write more and make sure I've done my best."

—Kara (Grade 6)

See Digital Task Card: Inspiration Scavenger Hunt on page 64.

Keep It Real

A group of Grade 4 students used a collection of images as the inspiration for creative writing. These students used a camera to take a series of pictures. They were then able to combine the pictures in a sequence that told a story. By adding text, they were able to write about things that are personally important and inspiring for them. By selecting images that were inspiring and unique, these young writers combined these seemingly random photos into a complete story.

Science Connection

Tech Tool: Digital Story
What is a digital story?
A digital story is a series of pictures that are combined with text to tell a story or share information.

Digital Task Card: Where You Live

Create a digital story that shows where you live.

Take pictures of different living things (plants, trees, animals, insects, etc.) and evidence of living things (nests, animal tracks, broken branches, etc.). Find out which creatures and plants live in your area. How can you find out more about these living things? Are there special features (adaptations) that help these things live in your area?

Use the Internet and nonfiction books to find out more about the habitats around where you live.

Combine the pictures with the information to make a digital story about the wildlife in your local habitats. What did you learn about the place where you live? Why is it important to protect the plants and animals around us?

Share your digital story with your friends.

Pembroke Publishers. © 2010 *Keepin' It Real* by Lisa Donohue. ISBN 978-1-55138-260-9

Writing Connection

Tech Tool: Digital Story
What is a digital story?
A digital story is a series of pictures that are combined with text to tell a story or share information.

Digital Task Card: Inspiration Scavenger Hunt

Go on an inspiration scavenger hunt.

Use a digital camera to take pictures of things that you find inspiring. Find things in your classroom, school, or community that interest you, challenge you, or confuse you. You can take pictures of things you find or ask your friends to pose for you. Try to capture the unusual, the unique, and the interesting.

Use the images you've captured as a source for inspiration in your writing.

- What stories do the pictures tell?

- How can you add your voice to the images?

- What details do you notice in the images that you can describe fully through your writing?

- What do you think happened before the picture was taken? What happened after?

You may choose to express your writing in the form of a narrative, a recount, a poem, a letter, or simply a caption.

Share your work with your friends. Did they see the same things in the pictures you took?

Pembroke Publishers. © 2010 *Keepin' It Real* by Lisa Donohue. ISBN 978-1-55138-260-9

Science Connection

Tech Tool: Prezi
What is a Prezi?
Prezi is an interactive presentation format. With a Prezi, you can create a project with infinite space; you can zoom into and out of images.

Digital Task Card: Substance Abuse

Use the Prezi presentation format to create a Public Service Announcement about the risks of substance use and abuse.

Use the Internet and other nonfiction resources to find out as much as you can about different substances (e.g., alcohol, illicit drugs, dangerous household goods, etc.). Find information that describes the risks and dangers of improper use or abuse.

Combine images and text to create a zooming presentation. You can choose to research as much as you can about one particular substance, or find out about many different substances.

Share your Prezi with your classmates. You might end up saving someone's life!

CHAPTER FIVE

Critical Literacy

"Giving students a chance to share their work with a global audience is an important first step, but there is much more to it. It's in the conversations, the links, and the networks that grow from them afterward that we really begin to understand the profound implications for lifelong learning."
—Will Richardson

You Don't Have to Agree with Me

Critical literacy is the ability to evaluate, analyze, and question texts. Readers who are critically literate are able to think about the content of a text and look for underlying meanings. Critical literacy allows readers to evaluate the intention behind text and to think, not only about making sense of the words on the page, but also about the deeper meaning behind them. Students who are able to read are able to make meaning from the text, but students who are critically literate think about the way it affects them. In order to think critically, students need to read, understand, evaluate, synthesize, and analyze. It is not sufficient to read and understand the content of a given text; instead, readers need to think about the messages contained in the work and compare those messages to their existing knowledge base, opinions, and beliefs.

"I like reading things that I can relate to. When I don't understand what a book is talking about, I don't want to read it anymore."

—Ricky (Grade 4)

Often we think of criticism as a fault-finding process. Critical literacy is not about finding fault; instead, it challenges students to delve into texts to find their deeper meaning. It encourages students to become reflective readers and thoughtful learners. Students are encouraged to consider different perspectives and to think independently about the information being presented. As students become more critically literate, they become independent-minded. They are able to assess information presented through texts and analyze the messages being presented. They are able to judge for themselves and think for themselves.

Critically literate readers are encouraged to formulate their opinion of texts. Students need to know that it is acceptable to agree or disagree with texts; just because something is written down, it is not necessarily correct. There are many times we encounter stereotypes, biases, or opinions in texts that may be different from the ones we personally hold. Readers who have a critical stance recognize that it is permissible to challenge these messages. Critically literate readers evaluate text through a "lens of truth." By reading through this lens, they are able to evaluate the underlying messages of a given text and to formulate an opinion. We want our children to question things and bring the passion of their opinions to discussions. We want students to agree and disagree with the text and with each other. Most of all, we want them to *think* about the things they read.

When students are critically literate, they are actively engaged with the text, rather than being passive observers. They are participating in an ongoing dialogue with the author of the text—posing questions, determining meaning, and thinking about the choices the author made. Students are encouraged to think independently and dig deeper, to go beyond the surface meaning of the text and looking for underlying messages. They are able to develop empathy for others, consider different perspectives, and express their own opinions with clarity and conviction.

Critical literacy is not a subject or strategy to be taught in isolation. It is a perspective with which students approach all texts and the world around them. If we truly want our students to begin to take a critical stance, it needs to become an embedded element of all literacy events. It needs to become a lens through which they view all texts.

We need to encourage our students to express their opinions and respect the opinions of others. This can happen only in a classroom environment where all students feel that their voice is valued and respected. All students should feel free to take risks as learners, pose questions, and state their opinions. They need to listen attentively to their peers and to agree or disagree respectfully. We need to provide our students opportunities to have ongoing conversations about important issues, and we need to help them to develop effective strategies for listening and responding to their peers.

What Makes a Text?

Text is not limited to the books we read, but is all around us. It is the way in which messages are communicated in our world. While books are important for developing and strengthening literacies, the world is full of other texts that we constantly read, interpret, and analyze. They may include articles in the daily newspapers, messages on billboards, information on the Internet, images in comics, the content of advertisements, slogans on products—and the list goes on. We live in a text-based world. It is ever-present in our culture.

We are surrounded by messages through a vast array of texts. We need to provide authentic opportunities for our students to interact with these different texts, so that they can develop an understanding of how they are created and take a critical stance when analyzing them. We need to include texts of different levels of difficulty and complexity. We need to introduce our students to different text forms on a broad range of subject matter. If we want our students to become critical thinkers, we need to provide them with opportunities to think about deep issues. They need to consider human issues, witness authentic global events, and evaluate ethical dilemmas. They need opportunities to read, reflect, and respond. Developing a culture of critical literacy invites students to question the content of texts, analyze the messages, and express their views on a wide range of issues.

Critical literacy becomes especially important when dealing with media texts. The intention of many media texts is to convey a strong message, challenge readers' perceptions, or alter their actions on an issue. When readers are critically literate, they are more able to think about the biases and underlying intentions behind the messages. They think about the audience, the message of the text, and the intention of the piece. Having your opinion changed by a media text is not necessarily a bad thing. For example, media texts that are intended to raise

"When I read stuff, I ask myself 'could that really happen?'"
—Emma (Grade 3)

awareness of important social issues (e.g., bullying) are created with the intention of changing others' thoughts and actions. As critically literate readers/viewers, we are more able to assess the message and determine if it holds true with the opinions we personally hold. If we disagree with the message being presented, we are challenged at a certain level to assess and perhaps re-evaluate our personal opinions based on the new information. As critically literate individuals, we have the opportunity to measure the message against our personal opinions. The text may serve to strengthen an already existing opinion or challenge it. We want our students to bring an openness of mind to their texts, but we also want them to know which beliefs they personally value.

Readers, Take Your Positions

We can help students to learn to think more critically about texts through a wide range of activities. As students deconstruct different texts, they begin to see how they work and fit together. They can identify the strategies used by authors and examine the effect they have. Students not only become critically aware of when an author is using these strategies to influence the way they interpret the information as readers, but also can think of how they can use these same strategies to influence others. They can become critically literate readers and critically aware writers. They discover how others try to influence them, and also discover how best to influence others.

Understanding Perspective

"There are two sides to every story," as the saying goes. But not every story provides an opportunity for us to see all sides. Most stories we read are written from the perspective of a main character, and the reader is influenced to see everything from this perspective. But there are other sides to the story, and critical readers must consider this: Whose sides? Whose voices have not been heard? Who has been silenced and whose story has not been told? Chances are, there are more stories hidden from view than the ones in the forefront. How can we draw our readers' attention to these hidden stories? How can we let them know that there are even more than two sides to every story?

Evolution in Action

After reading short stories, Farhana Panju wanted her students to consider the story from the perspective of the other characters. They began to dig deeper into the story, considering it from different perspectives, analyzing the bias of the author. The students developed arguments from the points of view of other characters, including opinions from characters that were initially silent. As the students began to see the other sides to the story, they evaluated the outcome of the story. Was it fair to everyone? Was it justified? Would the story have been significantly different if someone else was telling it? The students began to recognize the stories that had not been told, and compared them to the one that was. In this way, they began to have a deeper understanding of the text—and all of the stories within it.

See Digital Task Card: Captain's (B)log on page 75.

Keep It Real

Students in a Grade 6 class relished the opportunity to use new tools to learn about the past. For one such assignment, they decided to create a Captain's (B)log to document a European explorer's adventures. They created a blog and added entries, writing in role as the captain of the ship. They included accurate historical information (e.g., the size of the fleet, the direction traveled, the locations discovered), but also added their opinions, fears, and desires. They brought these historical figures to life! As the students worked on their captain's (b)logs, they began to gain a deeper insight into the realities of the early explorers. They commented on each other's posts and added their thoughts to their peers' work. As the students completed their work, they commented on the realities of the "human factor" with these historical people. They thought about the families these historical figures left behind, the frustration they would have felt, the fears they needed to suppress, and their approach to their crew. What better way to bring history to life than to give it voice?

Understanding Bias

It is very difficult to write an unbiased text. Most texts are written with some element of bias. Even this book: It is obvious that I believe that the new literacies are important, and I'm trying my hardest to convince you to agree with me.

Bias can be the particular slant an author takes, or it can refer to the way in which different people are portrayed. Understanding the author's bias helps the reader view the content of a text with a critical eye. When we evaluate different texts, we can think of biases that are intentional and biases that are unintentional. Authors might include information that will cause the reader to view the text in a certain light. This can be as simple as a character's role in the book, or as complex as the impact of different cultural groups in a story. When we begin to examine the stereotypes and biases in texts, it allows us to think more critically about the content the way in which it affects us, and the way we relate to the text.

Understanding Cause and Effect

Making connections within a text requires higher-level thinking skills. Readers need to determine the relationship between the events presented in a book. They need to see how things fit together. Students sometimes struggle to find the cause-and-effect relationships throughout a text. They are often blindsided by the outcome of a book because they never "saw it coming." Our young readers are often oblivious to literary devices like foreshadowing. They miss these subtle clues that help hold the plot together. Sometimes even the most obvious cause-and-effect connections are overlooked by our youngsters.

We need to encourage our students to look at a text as a unified piece of work. They need to find the links that hold it all together. We need to help them question the outcomes of books and to think about how the actions of characters brought about certain events. When readers interact with text in this way, they are thinking about the decisions the author made, questioning the actions of characters, and evaluating the events in the plot. When students begin to understand the cause-and-effect relationships, they will begin to think beyond the text. They can move from asking "Why did….?" to asking "What if…?" They can examine the different elements of a text, understand how they fit together, and imagine different outcomes.

Understanding Image

"A picture is worth a thousand words." Why? How? What kind of picture? Which words? Texts are rich with images that are carefully created or selected to convey a message. Images can be used to convey the mood of a piece, to draw the reader's attention to specific details, or to support the meaning of the text. Images can use a range of light and shadow, perspective, color, expression, or body language to communicate with the reader.

We need to draw our students' attention to images and the ways in which they are used to strengthen the author's message. Using the images, they can look for clues as to the mood of the piece, the focus of the writing, and the message the author is sending. They can think about the story that the pictures tell.

See Digital Task Card: Ancient Civilizations Scrapbook on page 76.

Keep It Real

Students in a Grade 5 class practiced their 21st-century scrapbooking skills as they collected images from ancient civilizations. Working in teams, these amateur archeologists collected images of different past civilizations (ancient Greece, ancient China, ancient Rome, ancient Egypt, etc). They found information and images that depict life during that time. They researched the hierarchy of power, typical dwellings, ancient relics, and other important cultural information. The students used a digital story as a way of combining the images and information. They shared their work with each other through their class website, and created a virtual museum of the ancient civilizations.

Understanding Author's Intent

Most texts are created for a purpose. There are many different reasons for an author to create a text. It might have been created with the intention of entertaining, informing, or persuading.

See Digital Task Card: Environment PSA on page 77.

Keep It Real

Students in a Grade 5 class became increasingly concerned with the environmental impact of recent global events. They saw pollution having a catastrophic impact on the waters of the planet, and were concerned about the depletion of the Earth's natural resources. They learned the differences between renewable energies and nonrenewable ones, and studied the pros and cons of each source of energy. They decided to create public service announcements (PSAs) that would encourage others to become more globally responsible. They each selected a different environmental issue and began to compile research on it. They collected information and images, and recorded corresponding audio clips. The students created multimedia persuasive glogs. They shared their work with their classmates, their school, and the surrounding community. These youngsters developed a deeper understanding of their responsibility as global citizens. Their work resulted in a neighborhood cleanup, a greater awareness of recycling in the school and community, and a day of tree planting.

The author may choose to use certain words to influence the way the audience will respond to the text. *Loaded language* is the use of words that are intended to create a strong emotive response in the reader. Authors can create sympathy, anger, repulsion, joy, or any number of responses through their writing. They carefully select words that will position the audience to see things in a certain way.

For example, a newspaper editorial can have a particular slant or bias. The reporter might wish to create a positive or negative response to an event, and use loaded language to do so. Words or phrases like "notorious," "disastrous," "shrouded in secrecy," "catastrophe," "daunting," "rampant," and "clear and present danger" bring about a negative response in the reader. On the other hand, words like "exceptional," "compassionate," "safe, nurturing environment," "revellers feeling high-spirited," and "to the rescue" bring about a positive response in the reader. The author might use key words that can influence the reader's interpretation of an event.

The way in which ideas are expressed determines the way in which the audience will react to it. When readers are aware of the author's intent, it becomes possible for them to know when an author is using loaded language to tap into their emotions. Introducing our students to this strategy not only enables them to recognize loaded language, but also encourages them to think of ways they can use it themselves. As young writers, they can experiment with different words and phrases as a way of conveying strong emotions in their writing. They can begin by identifying key phrases in different texts and analyzing the effect they have on the reader. Then can they try applying some of these strategies to their own writing.

See Digital Task Card: Hot Topic on page 78.

Keep It Real

The students in a Grade 7 class used a blog as a forum for discussing "hot topics." The students posted persuasive essays, clearly stating their opinions on important issues and relevant supporting evidence. They shared their blogs with their classmates and responded to the posts of others. Through this forum, they were able not only to discuss "hot topics" but also to notice techniques their peers used in their writing that made some communication more effective than others.

Critical Literacy in the Digital World

The digital world is full of texts that are intended to influence others. As wonderful as the Internet is, it is full of inaccuracies, misleading information, and hidden messages; all the more reason for us to help our students become critically literate. They need to realize that the openness of the Internet, which is its greatest asset, is also its greatest problem. The fact that anyone, anywhere, can create and post information means that anyone, anywhere, who has an opinion, bias, or hidden agenda can share these with the world. We need to be ever more savvy when reading and responding to information we encounter online. As crit-

"My teacher tells us to think when we read, but I think that it's more important to think *about* what we're reading."

—Sam (Grade 5)

ically literate Internet users, we need to pay particular attention to the source and intention behind every text we encounter.

Of primary importance is the source and form of text. We know that anyone can create a website or blog, and anyone can edit a wiki. We also know that images can be enhanced and manipulated. Thus, we need to help our youngsters identify reliable sources of information and determine how to critically analyze the things they encounter. When students are aware of the way in which texts are created, they become knowledgeable of the strategies others have used to create texts. When we introduce our students to digital tools like wikis, they begin to realize that anyone can alter the text. They begin to read with a more critical eye. They begin to think that, if they have the opportunity to manipulate the text, and they have the possibility of being wrong, perhaps the last person who edited the text may also have been wrong. We don't want our children to become cynical, disbelieving everything they encounter; however, we also don't want them to be gullible, believing everything they come across. They need to weigh the sources of information, the forms of text, and the content of the messages in order to evaluate the reliability of the material.

Likewise, web users need to consider the intention behind the information they are encountering. They need to think about the reason the piece was created and the bias the creator may have brought to it. They need to be aware of advertising and to know how to respond when they are prompted to supply personal information (name, e-mail address, etc.). They need to know what to do when pop-ups appear on their screen and how to react should they encounter inappropriate content. These are the realities of working in cyberspace. Although most Internet users' intentions are innocent, there are those whose are not. We need to teach our students to critically analyze the information they encounter and to think carefully about the information they provide. The best protection for our students is education. They need to know how to access reliable information on the Internet, how to decipher the form and source of the text, how to think about the intention of the piece, and how to respond appropriately. These are all critical literacies, and they are crucial in the digital world.

Linking the Literacies

The link between critical literacy and reading, writing, listening, and speaking is clear. As students develop their critical literacy, they begin to use their higher-level thinking skills. They engage with texts at a deeper level and they think more analytically about the messages they encounter and the messages they send.

Reading

Readers who are able to approach texts with a critical stance are better able to decipher implicit messages. They learn to read between the lines, see the hidden meaning, and make inferences. Critical literacy requires students to make connections within a text and to think about connections between the messages they encounter and their existing knowledge, beliefs, and opinions. It requires that they think about different biases, slants, or perspectives in texts. When readers are critically literate, they think about the relevance of information. Finally, critically literate readers recognize that messages can change, depending on the source.

Writing

As students learn to take a critical stance, they can transfer these skills into their writing. They can use voice in their writing to create a mood for their readers. They can choose words that strengthen the message they are trying to send. As they become aware of the ways in which different texts are created, they can apply this knowledge to the creation of their own texts. They can organize their information in ways that best represent the message they are trying to send; they can think about what they wish to include, emphasize, or leave out. They make informed decisions as writers, thinking about the ways in which they will affect their readers.

Listening and Speaking

Giving students opportunities to share their opinions with others enables them to listen attentively, speak respectfully, and articulate their ideas clearly. They need to learn to respect the ideas of their peers, even when they disagree. When students are given regular opportunities to share, debate, and defend their opinions, they become better at expressing their ideas, as well as responding to the ideas of others.

Social Studies Connection

Tech Tool: Blog
What is a blog?
A blog is a forum where one user can start a discussion and the other users can post replies.

Digital Task Card: Captain's (B)log

Use a blog to create a captain's (b)log.

Pretend that you are a captain of one of the early European explorers' ships. You can imagine that you are a famous explorer or a captain on one of the ships in his fleet.

Create a blog that includes at least three journal entries describing the things you might have seen and experienced on your voyage.

1. Think about your long trip across the ocean. Describe the way you felt as you faced the different perils along the way. What are some things you saw? How did you feel? How did the crew feel?

2. Describe your first impressions of the "new land." What did it look like when you first arrived? What plans did you have for this new place?

3. What happened when you discovered that there were people living in this "new land"? What was your first meeting like? How did they react to your presence?

Share your captain's (b)log with your peers, and encourage others to comment on your ideas.

Tech Tool: Digital Story
What is a digital story?
A digital story is a series of pictures that are combined with text to tell a story or share information.

Digital Task Card: Ancient Civilizations Scrapbook

Use a digital story to create a scrapbook of ancient civilizations.

Use the Internet and nonfiction resources (books, magazines, texts, etc.), to find out more about ancient civilizations. You can choose one specific civilization or find out about many of them. You might choose to research Ancient Greece, Ancient China, the Mayan Civilization, Ancient Egypt, Ancient Rome, or any other early civilization.

Find out as much as you can about ways of life in the civilization. Include specific information about homes, hierarchy of power, beliefs, traditions and rituals, architecture, etc.

Combine images with your research to create a digital story. Make sure that you respect copyright rules on images and text. You need to write your information in your own words and make sure that you have permission to use any Internet images you find.

Save and share your digital story with your classmates.

Pembroke Publishers. © 2010 *Keepin' It Real* by Lisa Donohue. ISBN 978-1-55138-260-9

Science Connection

Tech Tool: Glog
What is a glog?
A glog is a graphic blog. It is a way of sharing images, text, audio and video clips with others.

Digital Task Card: Environment PSA

Use a Glog to create a Public Service Announcement about the environment.

Think of a way to convince people that they need to be more responsible global citizens. You might wish to encourage people to recycle more, reduce their carbon footprint, or conserve energy.

Use the Internet or nonfiction resources (books, newspapers, magazines, etc.) to find out more about an environmental issue.

Share your ideas on a glog. You can include images, text, and audio or video clips. Remember to respect copyright on images and information. You need to write your ideas using your own words.

Once you've completed your Public Service Announcement, share it with your friends. Encourage them to comment on your work—and you can comment on theirs.

Pembroke Publishers. © 2010 *Keepin' It Real* by Lisa Donohue. ISBN 978-1-55138-260-9

Writing Connection

Tech Tool: Blog
What is a blog?
A blog is a forum where one user can start a discussion and the other users can post replies.

Digital Task Card: Hot Topic

Use a blog as a way of expressing your opinion on something you feel strongly about.

Make sure that you clearly state your point of view and provide enough supporting evidence to explain why you feel the way you do. You need to use a persuasive voice in your writing and try to convince your readers that your perspective is best.

Make sure you include a main idea, supporting details, and a concluding statement. You might choose to write a blog about any "hot" topic. Here are some suggestions:

- Kids should be allowed to listen to their MP3 players during class time.

- Kids should be allowed to chew gum at school.

- All sport clubs should be publically funded and free to all kids.

- Students should be encouraged to use computers more at school.

- All fast-food restaurants should include healthy choices.

- All citizens have a responsibility to reduce their carbon footprint.

Invite your classmates to read your blog and respond to your writing.

Pembroke Publishers. © 2010 *Keepin' It Real* by Lisa Donohue. ISBN 978-1-55138-260-9

CHAPTER SIX

Putting It All Together

"Technology is just a tool. In terms of getting the kids working together
and motivating them, the teacher is the most important."
—Bill Gates

Not *Why?* But *How?*

When I began my teaching career many years ago, I stood at the door of my
classroom every morning, welcoming my students into my room. It seems that
now I stand at my classroom door and, instead of inviting them in, I invite them
to look out, beyond our walls, beyond our community and into the world. The
digital age has brought about a radical change in the way we access, interpret, and
share information. We need to make sure that our classrooms are reflecting this
global transformation.

The new literacies are not optional. If we want our students to be proficient
readers, they must be digitally literate, media literate, socially literate, and critically literate. They must know how to access information through digital tools,
understand the social norms associated with Internet use, understand the way a
message can be presented through the different media, and think critically about
the content. Our readers regularly read a broader variety of text forms than even
existed when we were their age. The clear division between fiction and nonfiction has been blurred by a spectrum of forms and formats of text. Students need
to make sense of the words in order to decode and, in essence, to read. But this is
no longer sufficient for effective reading. Reading needs to refer to a deep understanding, a critical analysis, and a thoughtful evaluation of the messages contained within the words. Our readers can not be passive in the process. The text
they encounter demands more of them. They need the new literacies in order to
understand and respond to the vast array of new text forms.

Our young writers need a similar set of strategies. Writing no longer is simply
the process of putting pen to paper. Instead it can be redefined as capturing our
ideas in a way that we can share them with others. Students can "write" in many
different ways and using an enormous array of forms. We need to encourage our
students to explore the different ways of capturing their ideas—from "putting
pen to paper" to texting. Each form of text comes with its own set of norms and
conventions. As with reading, the number of forms of writing is as vast as the
formats in which we can write, and these forms include blogs, wikis, texts, chatrooms, instant messaging, and on and on. Students need to be exposed to this
array of text forms and need to realize that, when they are writing, context and
format are essential for determining content. They need to think critically about
the messages they are intending to send and the formats they are using to express

themselves. Students need to become versatile writers, adapting their skills to the demands of many different forms of writing. There is no way that we can realistically teach every form of writing; instead, we need to teach our students to evaluate new text forms they encounter, to think about the ways they are constructed, and to apply that thinking to their own writing. They need to learn to adapt their writing—both form and content—to the ever-changing demands of the digital world. The only way we can accomplish this is by providing them with many different opportunities to encounter new texts and to respond with writing of their own. They need to know how to write and respond in a digital world, they need to use social norms to share their writing and respond to the work of others, they need to understand how media texts work in order to create their own, and they need to think critically about their writing, using strategies to best communicate their messages to an audience. Our young writers need the new literacies too.

Listening and speaking are essential for face-to-face communication, but does that change when we enter the digital world? Again, the forms and formats in which we are required to listen carefully and speak clearly are widely diversified. In face-to-face communication, listeners have the opportunity to ask questions for clarification and speakers have the option of further explaining their ideas. This changes somewhat in the digital world. Often students encounter audio content that is pre-recorded and they need to listen, analyze, and evaluate the things they hear. Likewise, when they are sharing their work through audio or video posts, students need to recognize the importance of speaking articulately, with inflection, and with clarity of ideas. Students need to develop the skill of expressing their ideas in clear, concise ways. Their audio posts need to be engaging and yet succinct. The new literacies demand more from our students as listeners and speakers. They need to be active, analytical listeners and articulate speakers. Students need to use digital tools to listen, share, and respond to the work of others, They need to be socially aware, to consider the purpose of different media pieces and think critically about audio or video content.

The new literacies are everywhere. They are embedded in the old. For our students to be effective readers, writers, listeners, and speakers, they need to see these skills in the context of the new literacies. They need to read, write, and respond using digital tools, they need to participate as responsible global citizens, they need to create and analyze media texts, and they need to be critically aware of the information they encounter. Reading, writing, listening, and speaking are no longer entities of their own; they need to fit into the real world in which our students live.

Play with Purpose

"All texts require exploration, interrogation, elaboration, and interactive response modes that extend, expand, and enrich the experience of the text."

—David Booth (2008)

Through writing this book, I discovered more digital tools with which I was unfamiliar than ones I already knew about. When I encountered a new tool, the first thing I did was play with it. I needed to figure out how it worked before I was able to determine how I might use it in my classroom. This process also holds true for our students. When we introduce them to a new tool, we need to allow them some freedom to experiment with it. We need to give them a little creative license and to encourage them to figure out how the tool will work best for them. As with most digital technology, the beauty of the tool is in the versatility and creativity it allows its users. We need to introduce our students to these tools, and allow them the opportunity to explore and create with them.

Work with Tools

Digital tools are just that: *tools*. They are things that we can use to teach, learn, and communicate. It would be pointless to study the attributes of a hammer without thinking of the way we use it. A hammer is a simple tool but, in the right hands, it can be the essential component in building something significant. Likewise, digital tools can be extremely versatile and flexible, but they are just tools. It is our job as educators to determine how to use these tools in our classrooms. We need to show students that these tools are important and can be used to support their learning. We need to find creative, authentic, and engaging applications for them. They need to become an integrated component of our literacy instruction—not a separate entity. Students don't need to be taught how to use digital technology, but they do need to be taught what to do with it. They need to find the practical purpose for the tool, and that becomes our job.

Handing students a tool without showing them its purpose is a recipe for disaster. If you placed a hammer in the hands of a young child, ultimately someone would get hurt, something would get broken, and significant damage would be done. The digital world is exactly the same. If we put technology in the hands of our students without first showing them the ways in which they are to use it, it will no doubt end badly. Technology is not a subject—it is a tool. We need to use technology to support and develop the other literacies. Students need to understand how these tools are to be used in the context of authentic learning tasks. For example, we should not teach students how to create a podcast just for the sake of creating a podcast. A podcast could be the tool they use in order to share their response to a specific learning task. Likewise, students should not create a digital photo story for the sake of learning how to create digital photo stories. Instead they can use this tool as a way of sharing their research on a given topic. We should not teach technology; instead we need to use technology to teach and learn.

Baby Steps

There are countless digital tools available. There is no way that one person could be proficient at using all or even most of them. It's like the old joke: *How do you eat an elephant? One bite at a time.* The same is true for learning about the vastness of the digital world. As busy educators, our best approach is to choose one digital tool that we think would be a good start, introduce it to our students, and see how many different applications we can find for it. Students are hungry for digital technology. If we start with one tool and begin to develop a level of comfort with it, then perhaps we can begin to explore another tool or two. If we give our students all of the tools at once, not only will they be overwhelmed, but so will we be.

Choose a starting point. Choose one tool to try, and see how it fits into your literacy instruction. Work with your students to develop new and innovative applications for it as a way of supporting their learning. As you and your students develop greater confidence with digital tools, you will all become more tech-savvy. As you develop a greater awareness of digital tools, then you (and your students) can begin think backward. Think about the outcome you wish to achieve, then think about which digital tool would best accomplish this.

Throughout this book, there are a number of different digital tools introduced. Lets take a look at these tools, and consider ways they can be used to support students' learning.

Digital Tool	Suggestions for Classroom use
Chatroom: an online space where users can engage in a conversation.	Chatrooms can be used as the forum for any discussion that students may have face-to-face. Some of these discussions might focus around books they have read, math problems that they are working collaboratively to solve, or any learning discussion group.
Wiki: a simple tool that creates a document that can be accessed and edited by many users.	A wiki can be used for any shared writing assignment. Students work together to collaborate on the writing, each editing and contributing to a joint text. Some applications include a class newspaper, collaborative story writing, and sharing research assignments.
Blog: a forum where one user can initiate a discussion topic and other users can post replies.	A blog can be used for sharing and responding to any piece of work. Students can use blogs as a venue to post their writing and provide feedback to their peers. They might choose to write opinion pieces, post persuasive texts, or share any piece of research connected to their learning.
Digital Story: a series of images, combined with either written or oral text, that is used to convey a message.	Digital stories can be used to create picture books, for sharing research, to create Public Service Announcements or any other piece of work that blends images with text.
Website: an online space where different users can access and respond to information.	A website is the most versatile of all tools. Teachers can create their own websites as a way of sharing classroom news, providing links to other sites, posting student work, updating homework and assignments, and providing a place for students to "turn in" their assignments. Websites allow teachers and students to have all of their information in one place. A well-organized website can function as a virtual file cabinet of information, assignments, and links for students.
Glog: a graphic blog that allows users to layer images, text, video clips, and audio clips.	Glogs can be used for any media presentation. Students can use glogs to create posters or Public Service Announcements, to present research information, and to respond to the work of others.
Podcast: a series of digital audio or video recordings.	Students can use podcasts to create commercials or news broadcasts, to share their research information, or to record and share dramatic presentations (audio or video).

Digital Tool	Suggestions for Classroom use
Public Service Announcement: a commercial intended to raise public awareness or change attitudes about specific issues.	Public Service Announcements can be used as a way for students to raise awareness of social issues or global events. PSAs might be created to influence peers' choices with substance abuse, body image, bullying, etc.
Prezi: a non-linear presentation format that allows users to add images and text in indefinite space.	A Prezi can be used for sharing and presenting any information: research material, social issues, or other curriculum content.
Comic Creators: applications that allow users to create comic strips using a bank of images.	Students can use comic creators as a way of sharing ideas, opinions, or information in a graphic way. They can use humor to express a point of view on any given topic.
VoiceThreads: an online collaborative conversation tool.	VoiceThreads can be used as a forum for students to post and respond to any ongoing conversation about a given topic; e.g., curriculum-related material, social issue, or global event.
Tag Cloud: a graphic image created with words.	Tag cloud applications allow students to see visually which ideas/words they have most emphasized through their writing.
Online Book Clubs: social networking sites for readers.	Students can select books that they've read, post summaries, and give recommendations. They are able to create "friend lists" and engage in conversations with these friends about books.
Digital music mixing software: software that allows users to combine different music and sound loops to create original pieces of music.	Students can use this software to create original soundtracks to be used on their own or in combination with other tools. They might create music for a presentation, a slideshow, a digital story, a dramatic presentation, or a PSA. The possibilities are endless.

Integrate Technology? With WHAT Resources?

The reality that most schools face is that staying on top of the latest technological advances is a difficult and costly proposal. It seems that, as soon as a school is able to purchase enough of one tool to ensure equal access by all teachers and students, the tool is already obsolete. It seems like we're fighting a losing battle by trying to equip our schools with technology. Investing small fortunes in computers, only to discover that within a year they're already too slow to run the latest software or online tool, is a frustrating experience. But we need to find ways of integrating technology into our classrooms, despite the overwhelming challenges we may face.

I can state honestly, if you have access to one computer and that computer is able to access the Internet, the world is at your fingertips. It is possible to integrate technology into your literacy program on a consistent basis. The major mindshift is that we need to make is from *teaching technology* to *using technology to teach*.

Many schools have moved from having a designated computer period (e.g., every Wednesday after recess) to an integrated model of technology use. This turns technology from a subject to a tool. This makes sense if we want students to think about how to use computers to broaden their understanding of literacy. Literacy encompasses all forms of reading, writing, thinking, and responding. When we think of differentiating instruction for students, using a broad range of tools with which they can read, write, and respond only makes sense.

Let's face the realities of the classroom. With limited funds and limited resources, how is it possible to integrate technology into a literacy program? Lets look together at a number of possible scenarios.

One Classroom Computer

Help! I have one computer in the corner of my classroom. What can I do with one computer? How can I ensure that all of my students are given an opportunity to access this tool?

Working with only one computer is certainly a challenge, but not impossible. The best way of utilizing one computer is to use it as both an independent activity and a literacy work station. Debbie Diller's *Literacy Work Stations* has many helpful suggestions on how to create and implement these cooperative learning opportunities for students. If the computer is turned into a work station, students are given an equal opportunity to use the tool. Students can work independently or with a partner to share the resource.

If the computer is used twice a day during a literacy block (once during independent work time and once during literacy work stations), then it is possible for at least three students to access the computer—totalling at least fifteen students working on the computer in a week. At this rate, students will have access to the computer approximately once every two weeks. Although this is not the best scenario for digital integration, it is possible. Let's say that, during a typical 100-minute literacy block, students read/work independently for 30 minutes and work cooperatively for 20 minutes, allowing for two chunks of time at which students can use the computer. One such literacy block might look like this:

10 minutes – Word Skills (word work, etc)
20 minutes – Direct Instruction (e.g., modeled reading)
30 minutes – Independent Work Time/Guided Reading (independent reading, responding to reading, working on writing, independent computer time, etc.)
20 minutes – Direct Instruction (e.g., modeled writing)
20 minutes – Cooperative Learning Time (literacy work stations, shared computer activity)

While this example is just a suggestion of how a teacher might choose to utilize class time, it is the authenticity of the tasks students are working on that will determine their level of engagement and ultimately their learning. As teachers, we are known for finding creative ways of using the resources we have. Thinking about how to best incorporate technology might require not only creative thinking, but also creative scheduling. It is possible that we just need to think outside the box. We need to think beyond the typical constraints of the classroom and find innovative ways of doing things. Long gone are the days of classrooms filled with everyone doing the same thing at the same time. We need to provide a range of learning opportunities for our students, and the new literacies must be a part of this. When we have limited resources, we need to use them creatively, purposefully, and authentically.

See Digital Task Card: Create an Audio Book on page 89.

Keep It Real

In one classroom, the students have access to one iMac. The computer is a shared resource that all students are eager to use, and it is used on a daily basis by pairs of students. The work is arranged as a two-day station. On the first day, the partners meet to plan their ideas, choose a focus for their work, and divide the roles equally. One specific task requires students to use the PodCast feature to record a 30- to 40-second Breaking News Broadcast about a book they are currently reading. The first day of this station does not require access to the computer, so technically two groups are working on this station simultaneously: one group planning, the other actively recording. On the second day, the students use the computer to record their podcast, add special effects and music jingles, and save or share their work.

One computer can go a long way, if it is creatively used. Making the most of the station is crucial if students are to get the most out of it. We need to ensure that the task they are working on is authentic and purposeful. Think of ways in which the students can make the most of their time with this resource.

Computer Lab in the Library

How can I integrate technology when the computers are housed in a library?

If your computers are located in the library, spend some time with your teacher-librarian and find out if there are any times when the computers are not being used. Are there times when there are five or six computers free? This is important information when planning your literacy block. If you can schedule your literacy block during a time when a few of the computers are available, then they can easily become an integrated part of your literacy time. The demands on the teacher-librarian are forever increasing, so the last thing you want to do is impose further on his/her busy schedule. If your students are to use the computers in the library on a regular basis, you would need to spend some time ensuring that there is a mutually agreed-upon set of expectations for your students. These expectations need to be clear to the students, as well as shared by the classroom teacher and the teacher-librarian.

Building student independence by allowing students time to work in the library on the computers can be very empowering for youngsters. In this scenario, the computers become an activity during independent work time. The key to success with this approach is ensuring that students have sufficient choice in the tasks they are to complete on the computers, as well as the knowledge that they are accountable for completing certain tasks. Allowing students to just "use the computers" is a recipe for disaster. That is akin to saying that, during writing today, we're going to "use a pencil." If those instructions were given to students, it would result in all forms of doodling and "creative" uses of pencils. Some would take to writing on desks, some would try drawing on their books, some might even experiment, trying to poke the point of the pencil through a wide range of materials—including their own skin or the skin of others! I am certain that very little productive writing would result. Likewise, when we ask students to "use the computers," we need to be very specific about what they are using them for. This is especially important if we are asking our students to work relatively independently in a shared space like the library. When students are sent to the computers, we need to make sure that they understand what task they are being asked to complete. For example, students might be asked to use their time to complete a blog using a persuasive form of writing. This is not a time for surfing the Web or playing games. When students know that they are working with time constraints and clear expectations, they will be more likely to use their time in a focused, productive manner.

In order to avoid frustration for themselves and the teacher-librarian, students need to be grouped in ways that allow them to work productively together; consider including an "expert" in each group, who would be able to provide support to the other students should they encounter technical challenges or need clarification on the assigned tasks. When students are working out of our immediate view, we need to build in an element of accountability.

www.moodle.com

"By keeping all of our work in one place (our moodle), I know where to look to find anything important. All of my information is organized and I can find it, share it, and fix it."
—Andrew (Grade 5)

Keep It Real

One tool that teachers might find particularly helpful is a moodle. A moodle is a secure teacher-created website. It allows teachers to monitor and track participants' activities at any given time, from any location. Teachers are able to log on to the moodle and see exactly what their students are working on, what they have completed, and the work they have contributed. Teachers can easily create reports showing the length of time students have spent on each activity, which sites have been accessed, and the work they have done. If teachers use a moodle, students are aware of the teacher's ability to track their work from remote locations; they are aware that, even though they might be physically separated from their teacher, their activities are still within plain view. Perhaps this sounds a little like George Orwell's Big Brother, but the reality is that independence is best created under a watchful eye of a teacher. A little accountability goes a long way. Letting the students know that we are keeping our finger on the pulse of their learning ensures that they will use their independence appropriately.

This independent work time may be a part of students' regular daily routine, and is the key element in a balanced literacy program. Ensuring that students have strong independent work habits and are engaged in authentic tasks allows the teacher time for small-group instruction. Initially, consider creating a schedule that will serve as your guided reading schedule as well as your computer schedule. During independent work time, students can work independently on a number of tasks, one of which would involve the computers. Initially, students can work from a schedule. However, as students become more adept at using technology as a tool, they may be able to independently select which task they need to work at in order to complete all of the required jobs. One such list of tasks might look like this:

- Independent Reading
- Responding to Reading (due on Monday)
- Work on Writing
- Complete Online Blog (due Wednesday)
- Guided Reading
- Exchange a Book

In this example, students know that they are required to have their blog completed by Wednesday and their reading response completed by Monday. As students become more able to monitor their own learning and make decisions about how to manage their time effectively, they will be able to provide valuable input into the tools that they need access to. You might start the year using a computer schedule, but find that, as students learn to monitor their own progress, they will say things like, "I don't need the computers today, I finished my blog last week," or "Please, can I use the computer again today, I just need to add one more sentence," or "I don't want to use the computers today, I'm at a really exciting part of my book, and I'd like to keep reading." Being flexible with our students will help them make decisions that will enable them to take more ownership of their learning. When we include our students in decision-making, they will take more responsibility for their learning and ultimately become more independent learners.

Computer Lab

If your computers are housed in a separate lab or classroom, and you have an assigned computer period every week, then it is important that tasks are connected to the learning that is taking place in the classroom. The fact that the computers are physically separated from the classroom makes it difficult for students to see how their learning is directly related to their classroom experiences. As teachers, it is our responsibility to make these connections explicit. They need to know that the activities they work on in the lab are directly supporting the things they are learning in the classroom, and vice versa. Think of purposeful, engaging tasks for students that will help them make direct connections to their classroom experiences. Students could be working on any number of tasks—responding to reading, creating new writing pieces, developing a presentation that represents their research, responding to the work of others, or many other options.

A cow in the Classroom

If you are among the fortunate few who have access to a bank of laptop computers that are housed in a cart, then you should celebrate the opportunities for digital integration a Computer on Wheels (COW) brings! With as few as five or six computers, teachers can run a completely integrated digital literacy program. In a classroom like this, teachers can use the computers for independent and shared learning opportunities. Students are able to see direct connections between the skills they are learning in the classroom and how they are necessary in the world.

During independent work times, students can use the computers to read, write, and respond in a variety of ways. They can use digital tools to create and share their ideas, critically analyze information they encounter, and provide feedback to their peers. Independent tasks might include creating and responding to blogs or glogs; chatting in a literacy chatroom; editing or adding to a class wiki; researching and reading information; etc. Cooperative learning tasks might include creating a PSA; creating or responding to digital stories or VoiceThreads; using digital mixing to create a unique piece of music; developing an advertisement, news report, podcast, or any other media presentation; etc.

Regular integration of computers eventually robs them of their novelty. Students move quickly past the "play" stage and into authentic learning and application of the tools. The more students use technology, the more it becomes just another tool. Initially, they will all want the computers all the time. With a little structure, lots of authentic tasks, and lots of access, the computers will become a part of their learning.

Evolution in Action

Stephen Louca has never believed in reinventing the wheel, but he does think that at times it could use some rethinking. In his classroom, he enjoys taking tried-and-true techniques for teaching literacy concepts and applying a 21st-century spin to them. He also believes that the integration of technology holds the key to improving critical thinking and collaborative skills in his students. Stephen uses the interactive whiteboard in his classroom to this end. Teachers often give students cutout letters to manipulate so they can deconstruct words and learn to create new ones. In Stephen's class, students in small groups use the interactive whiteboard to manipulate letters, and then they collaborate to build upon each other's skills and to improve their own knowledge of words. The interactive whiteboard allows students to verify spelling and grammatical use by transfering the words immediately to a word-processing document where they can be used in sentences. Finally, students save the words to a shared file on the network that they can access on demand—a virtual word wall. Stephen's use of the interactive whiteboard is a great example of the power of integrating technology and its ability to improve collaboration and self-regulation.

Regardless of the way the technology is organized in your school, you need to find creative innovative ways of making it an integral part of your students' learning. The new literacies are here to stay, and we need to ensure that our students are as proficient with them as with the old literacies. It is impossible to teach reading, writing, listening, and speaking without teaching students what to read, write, and respond too. If they are not reading and writing with digital tools, then we are severely limiting them. A few years ago, educators recognized the importance of making the connection between reading and writing. Now, we must again push ourselves to make the link between the old and the new—between the foundations for learning and the application of it.

Reading Connection

Tech Tool: Podcast
What is a podcast?
A podcast is a series of digital audio or video recordings.

Digital Task Card: Create an Audio Book

Create a podcast that sounds like part of an audio book.

Select a book that you have recently read. Choose a really exciting part; write a script that includes the main characters and describes the things that are happening around them. Make sure to include clues to the setting of the story and enough information about the conflict in the story.

Ask your friends to role-play the different parts of the script and record their voices. Once you've recorded their voices, you can add special effects and music to help set the tone of the story.

Share your podcast with your classmates and invite them to comment on your work. Perhaps listening to your podcast will inspire them to read the book!

Pembroke Publishers. © 2010 *Keepin' It Real* by Lisa Donohue. ISBN 978-1-55138-260-9

The Final Word

As teachers, we are facing a constantly changing and evolving world. The demands on our time are phenomenal. We wear different hats and assume different roles every minute of every day. It's never easy to change the way we do things, especially when we've been doing something for a while. We are often comfortable with things the way they are, and change usually brings about uncertainty. Integrating new literacies into our classrooms might bring a variety of challenges, but it will result in countless rewards for our students. Every time we introduce something new, we face obstacles and difficulties, but we need to take the risk and do it anyway.

Through this book, you have been introduced to a wide variety of digital tools. My biggest piece of advice is this: Don't wait until you've figured it all out to try it. If we wait until we know everything there is to know about the new literacies before bringing them into our classes, we never will. This field is constantly evolving. New resources are being produced faster than we can imagine. We need to just jump in. I challenge you to become the biggest learner in your classroom. When we learn alongside our students, we encourage them to take greater risks, to work collaboratively as a learning community, to support each others' learning, and to apply their skills in new and innovative ways.

Acknowledgments

The concept for this book came upon me like a lightning strike. It was sudden, powerful, and perfectly clear. After listening to David Booth speak about the "new literacies," I was compelled to share ways in which we can integrate them into our classrooms. Thank you, David, for your passion, knowledge, and inspiration. Your vision for learning in the 21st century is revolutionary and dynamic.

This book could not have been possible without the collaboration of amazing educators who, on a daily basis, practice digital integration to the highest level: Royan Lee, who is leading the way with his 21st-century classroom; Jonathan Lewis, who embraces digital collaboration; Peter Jenkins, with his creative integration of new literacies; Arthur Birenbaum, for his expertise in social literacies; Don Kemball, who is eager to embrace new digital tools; Stephen Louca, a digital integration expert and "tech guru"; and Farhana Panju, for her undaunted enthusiasm and conviction for digital learning. A special thanks to Farhana for her contribution to this book through her support as my research assistant.

I am forever thankful for the school, community, and school board in which I work. It is an honor to be a part of such a forward-thinking educational community, where the new literacies are supported and embraced. I am truly appreciative of Michael Cohen, my principal, who not only provides us with the tools to be successful, but also allows us the freedom to use them fully. Michael has created a school climate where the new literacies are so intricately woven into the fabric of the school's culture that it is impossible to separate where the "old" meets the "new."

A special thank you to Deb Kitchener and the amazing champions of Learning Connections. Through this digital network I have met dedicated, innovative professionals who are creatively bringing the new literacies to life in their classrooms. Thanks for sharing your journey with me.

As always, thanks to Mary Macchiusi and Kat Mototsune, who share my vision for writing: Mary, who has recently become my head cheerleader (an honor once held by my mom); and Kat, my trusted writing coach and editor. I appreciate the constant feedback, gentle guidance, and prompting that enables me to write with conviction and clarity.

Most importantly, a special thanks to my family: Mike, Matthew, Hailey, and my dad. Mike, for his new-found cheerleading skills (and, as always, as snack-provider); Matthew and Hailey, for not jumping on me too much while I was trying to write; and Dad, for listening to huge chunks of text as I read this book aloud and reworked it in my mind. We can all celebrate as yet another book has reached completion.

Professional Resources

Booth, D. (2008) *It's Critical*. Markham, ON: Pembroke Publishers.

Booth, D. (2009) *Whatever Happened to Language Arts?* Markham, ON: Pembroke Publishers.

Bitner, Noel & Joel "Integrating Technology into the Classroom: Eight Keys to Success" *Journal of Technology and Teacher Education*, Vol. 10, 2002.

Carter, Jimmy (1998) *The Virtues of Aging*. New York, NY: Random House.

Coiro, J. (2009) "Rethinking Online Reading Assessment" *Educational Leadership*, 66(6), 59–63.

The Critical Thinking Consortium http://www.tc2.ca/wp/

Curriculum Services Canada, "Critical Literacy" *Webcasts for Educators* http://www.curriculum.org/secretariat/november29.shtml

Davis, A. P. & McGrail, E. (2009) "The Joy of Blogging" *Educational Leadership*, 66(6), 74–77.

Dewey, John (1944). *Democracy and Education*. New York, NY: Macmillan.

Diller, Debbie (2003) *Literacy Work Stations: Making Centers Work*. Portland, ME.: Stenhouse.

Eisner, Elliot W. (2003) "Preparing for Today and Tomorrow" http://www.hawken.edu/pdf/eisner.pdf

Mohr, M. & Orr, J. (2009) "Reader Responsiveness 2.0" *Educational Leadership*, 66(6).

Mustacchi, J. (2009) "R U Safe?" *Educational Leadership*, 66(6), 78–83.

Pahl, Kate & Rowsell, Jennifer (2005) *Literacy and Education: Understanding the New Literacy Studies in the Classroom*. London, UK: Paul Chapman Publishing.

Pink, Daniel (2005) *A Whole New Mind: Moving from the Information Age to the Conceptual Age*. New York, NY: Riverhead Books (Penguin).

Prensky, Marc (2001) "Digital Natives, Digital Immigrants" in *On the Horizon*, NCB University Press, Vol. 9, October.

Ramaswami, R. (2008) "The Prose of Blogging (and a Few Cons, Too)" *THE Journal*. Retrieved from: http://thejournal.com/articles/2008/11/01/the-prose-of-blogging-and-a-few-cons-too.aspx?sc_lang=en

Ray, J. (2006) "Welcome to the BLOGOSPHERE: The Educational Use of Blogs (aka Edublogs)" *Kappa Delta Pi Record*. Retrieved from http://findarticles.com/p/articles/mi_qa4009/is_200607/ai_n17184379/?tag=content;col1

Richardson, William (2009) *Blogs, Wikis, Podcasts and other powerful Web tools for classrooms* (Second Edition). Thousand Oaks, CA: Corwin Press.

Shea, Virginia, (1994) *Netiquette*. San Francisco, CA: Albion Books.

Texas A&M University–Corpus Christie, "Using Wikis as Collaborative Writing Tools" *Kairos 10.1* http://english.ttu.edu/kairos/10.1/binder2.html?http://falcon.tamucc.edu/wiki/WikiArticle/Home

Toffler, Alvin, Toffler, Heidi & Gibson, Rowan (1999) *Rethinking the Future*. London, UK: Nicholas Brealey Publishing.

West, K.C. (2008) "Weblogs and literary response: Socially situated identities and hybrid social languages in English class blogs" *Journal of Adolescent & Adult Literacy*, 51(7), 580–588.

Zawilinski, L. (2009) "HOT Blogging: A Framework for Blogging to Promote Higher Order Thinking" *The Reading Teacher*, 62(8), 650–651.

Index